MOBILITY AND IDENTITY
A STUDY OF JAT SIKHS IN CHANDIGARH

PRIYA KHANNA MAHAJANI

Copyright © 2014 by Priya Khanna Mahajani.

ISBN: Softcover   978-1-4990-9009-3
             eBook   978-1-4990-9008-6

All rights reserved. No part of this book may be reproduced or transmitted in any form or by any means, electronic or mechanical, including photocopying, recording, or by any information storage and retrieval system, without permission in writing from the copyright owner.

Any people depicted in stock imagery provided by Thinkstock are models, and such images are being used for illustrative purposes only.
Certain stock imagery © Thinkstock.

This book was printed in the United States of America.

Study was conducted between 1999-2001 and data was collected between May 2000 and July 2001.

Rev. date: 04/14/2015

To order additional copies of this book, contact:
Xlibris
0-800-056-3182
www.xlibrispublishing.co.uk
Orders@xlibrispublishing.co.uk

DEDICATED TO MY MOTHER

ACKNOWLEDGEMENTS

This research work has been completed under the supervision of Dr Surider S. Jodhka between 1999 and 2001 in Panjab University, Chandigarh. This work would never be what it is today without his constant and immensely valuable guidance. His patience and confidence in me pushed me ahead when I tended to slacken and enthusiastically encouraged me. He kept telling me that I was doing a great job and would definitely contribute something for the society, especially in this field of sociology. I was inspired to get this book published now and share my findings with all as I haven't been able to find any other study similar to mine that aims to explore and identify the reasons for mobility and its impact on identity among Jat Sikhs.

I'm especially thankful to my respondents, whose names I cannot mention due to confidentiality and various other reasons. They not only answered my questions with outmost patience, but also introduced me to other respondents and opened my eyes to several aspects of their lives that eventually found their way into my work. I am also grateful to them for their hospitality.

Last but not the least, I am thankful to my dearest father, Mr Subhash Khanna, who believed in me and gave me a vision to write this book, and my two sisters, Payal and Simmi, my husband Kedar Mahajani, and two lovely kids Riva and Arya for extending all the support and strength to be able to continue with the work and publication of this book. Without their love, affection, and constant motivation, I could not have completed this work. Their unflinching support and concern during my research work was a source of great inspiration and enthusiasm.

(Priya Khanna Mahajani)

CONTENTS

CHAPTER	TITLE	PAGE NO.
Acknowledgements		v
List of Tables		viii
Chapter – I	Introduction	1-17
Chapter – II	Methodology	18-23
Chapter – III	Jats in Chandigarh: The Social-Economic Background	24-42
Chapter – IV	Jats in Chandigarh: The Rural Linkages	43-62
Chapter – V	Jats in Chandigarh: Changing Life Styles and Identity	63-94
Chapter – VI	Summary and Inferences	95-104
	Bibliography	105-107
	Interview Schedule	108-112

LIST OF TABLES

Table No.	Headings	Page No.
3.1	Age of the Respondents	26
3.2	Family Occupation	27
3.3	Socio-Economic Class	28
3.4	Number of Houses Owned in Punjab	29
3.5	The Type of Residence	30
3.6	Members Staying in the Family	31
3.7	Assets Owned by the Family	33
3.8	Earning Members in the Family	35
3.9	Number of Students in the Family	36
3.10	History of Migration	38
3.11	The Area of Migration from Punjab	39
3.12	Type of Migration	40
3.13	Motivating Factors for Migration to Chandigarh	41
4.1	Acres of Agricultural Land Owned	45
4.2	House Owned in the Village	46
4.3	Mode of Cultivation of Land	47
4.4	Agricultural Land Sold in Last 10 Years	49
4.5	Agricultural Land bought in last 10 years	49
4.6	Source to Buy more Land	60
4.7	Money invested in after Selling Land	51
4.8	Number of Acres of Land sold in Last 10 Years	52
4.9	Number of Acres of Land bought in Last 10 years	53
4.10	Dependence of Income from Land	53
4.11	Visits to the Village	55
4.12	Settling Down in Village	56
4.13	Children to keep the village connections alive	57
4.14	Children to Carry on Agriculture	57
4.15	Positive Qualities of Rural Life	59
4.16	Negative Qualities of Rural Life	61

5.1	Educational Qualifications of the Resp.	67
5.2	Number of Years in Chandigarh	68
5.3	Preference for Occupation (Self)	70
5.4	Positive Qualities of Urban Life	72
5.5	Negative Qualities of Urban Life	74
5.6	Children to Marry According to their Wishes	76
5.7	Ideas Regarding Dowry	78
5.8	Appropriate Age for Girls to Marry	79
5.9	Appropriate Age for Boys to Marry	80
5.10	Ideas about gender Equality	81
5.11	Self identity on the basis of gender	83
5.12	Qualities preferred in the spouse	85
5.13	Identity Preference for self in Village	87
5.14	Identity Preference for self in City	89
5.15	Caste Identity in City	91
5.16	Religious Identity in City	92
5.17	Class Identity in City	93

CHAPTER 1
INTRODUCTION

Social mobility is an important aspect of the process of social change in developing countries like India. As the economy modernises, people tend to change their occupations and also move from rural to urban areas.

There has been a long tradition of studying the processes of social mobility in the discipline of sociology. Sorokin's, *Social Mobility* was published in 1927. His work is currently regarded by the students of social mobility as a pioneering study. According to him, 'social mobility is understood by any transition of an individual, or social object, or value from one social position to another' (Sorokin, 1959; p:133).

One of the conceptions of social transformations views modernisations as a process by which agrarian societies become wealthy industrial nations. This obviously implies a dichotomy of agrarian and industrial societies with its focus on industrialisation as a generic source of modernisation (Sharma, 1988 p:22).

As per this perspective, mobility takes place due to industrialisation, that is, people move from agrarian-based rural societies to industrial urban societies. In modernisation theory, this view of mobility is understood in terms of mobility in one direction only, that is, from rural to urban, traditional cultures to modern or secular societies. People not only change their occupations, but they also experience a complete change in their lifestyles and values. However, this has happened neither in the west nor in India. Even in the United States, which was predicted to be a melting pot; studies have shown that ethnic identities have been much too strong or significant to have melted in the national pot (Glazer & D. P. Maynihan, 1975).

Blua and Duncann (1967) were chiefly concerned with the process involved in the inter-generational transmission of status. Their interest in social mobility was restricted to determining the actual status of individuals. Hope (1974) devoted his efforts to the constructions of a multidimensional model for the study for mobility. Boudon (1973–74) was most concerned to explain that individual mobility was changing by relating it to the mechanisms generating inequality of educational structure. These mechanisms were defined on a macro-social level.

Studies of social mobility have mostly involved investigation into individuals (until recently only men's) change of occupation. Despite many claims to the contrary, group mobility, that is shifts by whole sections of society, is not taken into consideration within mainstream studies of social mobility.

The studies of mobility, regardless of how they are conducted and presented, rely on the concept of occupational hierarchy; thus, showing a vertical or upward or downward mobility. To study social mobility within the scope of a defined occupational hierarchy is undoubtedly to adopt a 'distributive approach' to sociological phenomenon (Sorokin, 1959).

In distributive conception of structure, the term 'social mobility' has a precise meaning. Mobility means a change in the possession of attributes on goods. Through mobility, individuals obtain or loose certain attributes or features.

Relational theories of structure are based on the concept of social relations. To date, the social relations approach has hardly been applied to the study of mobility. We only have some criticisms of mobility studies, focusing on the researcher's reluctance to examine the relational aspects of social life (Charvat et al., 1975; Bortaux 1976, 78). The main task facing investigations of mobility is to understand the individual and social aspects of current changes in society.

Karl Marx and Max Weber are the two great theorists whose work continues to inspire the relational conception of social structure (Marx, 1967, Marx and Engles, 1959, Weber, 1948, 68). Similarly

Giddens (1973) too rejects any conceptions of social structure as a reality external to processes of mobility (Giddens, 1973; p:20).

In mobility studies guided by Marxist thought, culture ought not to be considered as a mental category. Symbolic culture is strongly linked with occupational training and with the normative order. It is a means of 'cultural domination' (Archer and Vanghan 1971). It is this type of culture which differentiates between opportunities for mobility within the structures of classes and strata. It may be created, nurtured, and transmitted from one generation to another.

Bourdieu (1964) and Bourdieu and Passeron (1977) have argued that educational systems tend to stabilise the 'cultural capital' acquired mostly in the home. The concept of 'cultural capital' has been found very useful by the 'new' educational sociology in Britain (Karabel and Hasley, 1977, p. 41–61). What they propose is not to accept these about cultural capital but rather to test these theses within research into social mobility.

The concept of class domination is also of value to mobility studies. It highlights the way in which the structure or class strata manifest its existence in the organisational aspect of social systems.

SOCIAL MOBILITY IN INDIA

The studies on social mobility in India have been based on the horizontal or vertical mobility, that is, from rural to urban areas or change of caste into class. V.S.D' Souza, K. L. Sharma, M. N. Srinivas all have talked about the mobility of caste system into class system in India. According to D'Souza, 'the class is replacing the caste and the individual is replacing the group.' According to Srinivas, sanskritisation was the only way to remove impurity or to minimise it from the society. Therefore by this process, the whole community moved upward in the traditional caste hierarchy (Sharma, 1986; p. 35–44).

Emphasis on study of social mobility in terms of upward movement in caste hierarchy further legitimates the 'culturological' approach to the study of society. The concepts of dominant caste and sanskritisation show the possibility of corporate mobility in India (ibid.).

MOBILITY AND IDENTITY

Social mobility also implies change in identity, that is, from caste to class, from community to individual, or from caste to community. The problem of identity is not peculiarly modern. It is almost as old as recorded history. The Bible also contains many instances of concern with ethnic and social, individual, and collective identity. Ancient Greek mythology, too, reveals a strong interest in problems of social identity. According to Harris, there are generally two problematic questions (a) who am I? (b) What am I? Here, first one is generally answered by an assertion of continuity through genealogy and residence, the second by an assertion of distinctiveness through culture and community (Harris 1995).

According to Harris (1995), many philosophical problems about identity concern the criteria for the identity of particular things. Identity question can move very quickly from the seemingly trivial and verbal to the generally puzzling, and this fact itself is revealing. An essential part of the idea of social identity is that a particular human being can find or loose identity in social groups (Harriss 1995). Henry Tajfel, the founder of modern social identity theory, defined social identity as 'the individual's knowledge that he or she belongs to a certain social groups together with some emotional or value significance to him or her or the group membership' (Harris, 1995).

PERSPECTIVES ON IDENTITY

In the conventional sociological literature, there have been two perspectives to look at the identity. The first perspective is the social psychological perspective which deals with the self- identity and individualism. Mead and Cooley are the two scholars who have given the development of self -theory. According to 'the looking-glass self' theory of Cooley, he has focused upon the theory of social self, that is, the meaning of 'I' as observed in daily thought and speech. This mental picture of self is what Cooley called the 'the looking-glass self. For Cooley, social life is empirical self. To be aware of oneself was to be aware of society, 'self and society are twin born.' An individual's awareness of himself is a reflection of his perceptions of other's ideas of who he is, a process of one mind responding to other minds (Harlambos, 1980).

According to Mead, through the process of role taking, the individual develops concepts of self. The notion of self is not inborn, and it is learned during childhood, that is, in two stages: (1) play stage (2) game stage. Self is made up of the 'I' and the 'me'. The 'I' represents the impulsive tendencies and the component of self, the internalised demands of society. In short, as a 'me', the individual is aware of himself as a subject. One of the functions of self is to furnish the self-identities. In the process of social action and experience, the self receives the labels' names and other aspects of identity which others have for us and transforms them as our own. The self- organises the knowledge of 'who we are and what we think of ourselves in terms of our perceptions of other's responses.' Thus, the individual comes to think of himself as 'shy,' 'handsome,' or 'timid' because these are precisely the labels which he thinks the social world has attributed to him (Ibid.).

The second perspective is the social political notion of 'identity'. In this, identity is seen as source of collective mobilisation in terms of urbanisation, neighbourhood formations, vote banks, social movements, etc. Stuart Hall also identifies two different ways of thinking about identity. The first position defines cultural identity, in terms of one shared culture, 'a sort of collective one true self,' hiding inside the many other were superficial or artificially imposed 'selves,' which people with a shared history and ancestry hold in common. The second is an open-ended view of cultural identity. Cultural identity is a matter of 'becoming' as well as 'being'. It belongs to the future as much as to the past. It is not something that already exists, transcending pace, time, history, and culture. Cultural identities come from somewhere, have histories, and undergo constant transformations (Hall, 1990: 225).

Rayaprol (1997) has also talked about social mobility and identity in her book, **Negotiating Identities: Women in the Indian Diaspora**. She has studied the Indians settled in west and how religion helps them to preserve their individual self-awareness. Social mobility is a self-imposed exile for the increasing number of middle-class professionals, driven by economic and social aspirations. For these migrants, identities and cultures get delocalised, but they rarely get detached from the memories of past places and times. They evoke the past in highly selective ways and construct a present that is a hybrid of multiple cultures and experiences. According to Gillis.. (1994), identities and memories get transformed over time and, as a result, they tend to be subjective constructions of reality rather than objectively fixed phenomena (Rayaprol, 1997).

Rayaprol has also mentioned in her book that the major symbolic resource used by many migrants in the rebuilding of community is religion. It provides a powerful means to preserve and reinforce identities. Religion is one of the identity markers that helps people to preserve their individual self-awareness and group cohesion (Ibid).

Referring to the phenomenon of ethnic identities in the Indian context, Punakar (1947) has identified caste, language, region, and religion as the four major premises where ethnicity operates in a significant way. Ethnicity appears to operate through fission and fusion at different levels under diverse interactional situations (Bhat, 1983). Ethnic identity is the root where the interaction manifesting ethnicity stems from. Identity reflects both likeness and uniqueness.

It relates to that which the members of group share in common that, at the same time, differentiates them from 'others'. While some scholars consider that the various attributes constituting the 'ethnic' phenomenon are culturally defined, others argue that they are derived from common descent (Shibutani and Kwan, 1965; Schormerhonb, 1970).

From their review of work of ethnicity and ethnic group, Glazer and Moynihan (1975:4) concluded that ethnic groups in contemporary sociological thinking relate to all groups of society 'Characterized by a distinct sense of difference owing to culture and descent'. Weber (1965:306) included common experience under colonisation or migration besides descent and customs when he defined ethnic groups. This ethnic phenomenon gives rise to 'esprit de corps' among the members of a group which lends it a distinct identity. These identities are expressed and maintained by a name, shared beliefs and symbols, and projection of a distinctive lifestyle. Ethnic identity, besides providing an individual or a group requisite, has an interaction through identification, differentiates individuals or groups outside the purview. The identity of an ethnic group or its members is not just a case of self-identity but an identity which 'others' concede vis-à-vis- their own. (Bhat, 1983; p. 21–23).

THE JAT SIKHS OF PUNJAB

The Jat Sikhs constitute the main dominant caste in the countryside of Punjab. They enjoy the attributes of dominance, ownership and control of land, numerical preponderance, high caste status, reputation for aggression, predominant control of positions of power in Panchayati Raj institutions, co-operatives land mortagage, banks legislative, army, police and bureaucracy, etc.

Pettigrew (1975) observes that 'The Jats have formed the backbone of the agricultural community in Punjab. They divide themselves into a member of classes known as "got" each of which has a tradition of descent from a Rajput ancestor.'

Kaur, in her paper 'Jat Sikhs: a question of identity', has mentioned that the upward mobility of Jat Sikhs had begun in the time of Guru Gobind Singh, when large number of those baptised were Jats (Kaur, 1986).

The majority of Jat Sikhs belong to the rural areas of Punjab, and most of them are agriculturalists. The other occupation is they join the army. They have a tradition of serving the nation. They are considered to be one of the enterprising people who do not hesitate to migrate in search of work. For the Jats, it seems that there is an equal emphasis on the Jat (caste) part of the identity and also on occupation and ownership of land. The Jat might be employed as a school teacher or serve in the military, but he sees his primary role as that of an agriculturalist, his connection with land is what he holds most dear and what identifies him (Kaur, 1981–82). Pettigrew too similarly observed that the Jats despised 'the townsman as lacking in physical bravery. They also had an image of them as grasping greedy and lacking in dignity' (Pettigrew, 1975).

Many changes have been brought about in the Punjab countryside by the green revolution. The growing use of high-yielding varieties of seeds, fertilisers, pesticides, pump sets, marketing, etc has led to a large number of changes in the countryside. Punjab has emerged as the leading state of the country in terms of the highest per capita income.

However, a lot of controversy has been generated regarding the trickle-down effects of green revolution. The large landowning farmers obviously gained from this and found themselves with agricultural surpluses in hand, in a position of power and prestige. But, many have argued, this combat with new technology has been a losing battle for the small and the marginal farmers.

In rural life, those who benefited from the new technology and generated surplus did not, with their future generations, continue working as agriculturalists. Not only did they buy Maruti Cars and all the consumer goods that signified the lifestyles of the urban middle classes, but many of them also sent their children to study in the urban schools so that after being educated, they could find jobs in the urban sector (Jodhka, 1999; p:24).

According to Sucha Singh Gill, 'with the penetration of Capitalist relations in agriculture, modern education has spread. Most of the Punjab villages have schools and some even has colleges functioning in them. Some of the Capitalist farmers . . . are actually sending them to urban centres to acquire better education. With this a large number of educated persons from rural areas have been coming forward to take up jobs in government and semi-government institutions and departments. This has produced a distinct category of middle class intellectuals of rural origin' (as in Jodhka, 1999; p: 24).

An often ignored aspect of the green revolution has been its consequence at the cultural level, a point which has been put up by Shiva. According to her, commercialisation led to a complete erosion of the old value system. It altered the ethos of people in terms of value attached to money, profits, success, etc. It reflects a tendency of having high aspirations, not to accept low-paid jobs, of less-status and seek routes towards easy money and quick rich formulas, which brought more status as well as financial success (Shiva 1997).

The recent crisis of agriculture and spurt of suicides by farmers in Punjab has taken away the charm that agriculture enjoyed in Punjabi culture. It is not surprising therefore that in Punjab, today, no one celebrates agriculture. Therefore, people have started moving from rural areas where agriculture was practiced as the main occupation to urban and modern societies in search of middle-class occupations (Jodhka, 1999).

FOCUS OF THE STUDY

It is in this context that a study of the Jat migrants to Chandigarh and their changing patterns of identification become important and relevant. As mentioned above, the people of Punjab have always very closely identified themselves with rural and agrarian setting, particularly the dominant caste of Jat Sikhs. But economic prosperity has also led to mobility of people from rural to urban setting in search of further prosperity and middle-class occupations.

Though it has still not been quantitatively estimated, and proportionally its size may not be very high, the number of those who have migrated from rural areas to towns of Punjab in research of middle-class urban occupation is definitely quite large in absolute terms. The old assumption about the Jat Sikhs being a rural/agrarian caste and the Khatris and Aroras forming the urban middle class among the Sikhs no more holds good in contemporary Punjab. Although there has been some literature that talks about this type of mobility, their focus has remained on the economic process. However, economic change is also accompanied by cultural shifts.

Kaur, in her study of the Jat Sikhs' identity in rural Punjab, had observed that while in the village, at the village level, the Jat did not feel a threat to their identity; however, beyond village, especially at the regional and the national level, their concerns became the same as those of the urban Sikhs. Such an observation provides interesting implications of 'urbanisation' of the agrarian rich (Kaur, 1986).

It is in the context that a study on Jat Sikhs who migrated to Chandigarh becomes significant. It attempts to look at the changing notions of identity among the Jat Sikhs, both men and women. In the same context, the study of factors which largely provided the impetus for the Jat Sikhs to migrate to Chandigarh, their changing ideas of rural life, related issues of negotiating with caste and religious identities, and ideas regarding masculinity and feminity becomes relevant.

RESEARCH QUESTIONS

The empirical study of the Jat Sikhs in Chandigarh was carried out with the following objectives or research questions:

1. Patterns of mobility in the family of the migrants.
2. Changing attitudes of Jat Sikhs towards rural life and notions of rurality.
3. Their aspirations in relation to the nature of jobs and lifestyle.
4. The manner in which they negotiate their caste, class, and religious identities in the urban social context.
5. Their changing notions of masculinity and feminity?

The thesis has been divided into the following chapters.

The second chapter is on methodology and deals with the methods and techniques used for the study. The data was collected by using the interview schedule. Personal observations were also used to supplement the information particularly for explanations after study.

The third chapter is on the socio-economic background and mobility patterns of the residence. The chapter focuses on the age, income, occupation, reasons for migration to Chandigarh, type of migration, and the related issues.

The fourth chapter discusses the continued rural linkages of the Jat Sikhs in Chandigarh. In this chapter, issues relating to the contacts maintained with the village from where the respondents migrated have been discussed.

The fifth chapter focuses on the changing lifestyles and identity of the Jat Sikhs in Chandigarh. This chapter deals with the changing notions of lifestyle and identity among the Jat Sikhs as a result of mobility, viz. horizontal and vertical. It also lays an emphasis on the changing attitudes and self-perceptions regarding identity.

In the concluding chapter, an attempt is made to conclude and summarise the data collected, and inferences are drawn.

CHAPTER 2
METHODOLOGY

As mentioned in the first chapter, the major emphasis of this study is to look at the changing nations of identity among the Jat Sikhs migrants in Chandigarh. In this context, factors like what provided impetus to their migration to Chandigarh, their changing ideas of rural life, related issues of negotiating with caste, class, and religious identities, and ideas regarding masculinity and feminity becomes relevant.

SELECTION OF THE STUDY AREA

The Union Territory of Chandigarh, which is also the capital of Punjab and Haryana, is a likely choice for the prosperous Jats to settle down when they wish to move out of the village. Chandigarh is acclaimed as a modern and planned city. The other important factors that give Chandigarh strategic advantage in luring migrants include it being an important educational centre with a large number of schools, professional colleges, and the Panjab University. It is also known to be a heaven for the retired bureaucrats, government servants, and defence personal. It serves as an important centre for employment, particularly in the territory section. The other factors like the Punjab and Haryana High court, good shopping places, and a neat and clean environment also motivate people to choose Chandigarh as a destination.

RESPONDENTS

As the study is aimed to find the mobility pattern and changing notions of identity among Jat Sikhs, the empirical research was restricted to Jat Sikhs who had migrated to Chandigarh either for the purpose of education or occupation or for permanent settlement. The method of purposive case studies was used for the collection of data. In explicit terms, this method helped me to identify migrants from among those whom I was able to locate by my own social contacts and resources. These initial contacts then referred me to other migrants.

It was felt that given the limitations of time and resources available to an M. Phil student, a total of sixty case studies were thought to be of a reasonably manageable size. Both male and female migrants were interviewed in equal numbers to know their ideas regarding the questions asked. The respondents interviewed were between the age group twenty and forty years as the study aimed to find the changing notions of identity among the young migrants from different areas of Punjab and nearby place to Chandigarh.

PREPARATION OF THE SCHEDULE

For the purpose of collecting data, an interview schedule was made …..that included use of both structured and unstructured questions were …was prepared. The schedule was divided into eleven main parts. The first part elicited information about the socio-economic level of the respondent. In this, self-information about the family occupation, educational qualifications, age, socio-economic class, houses owned in Punjab, members residing in the present house, and the assets owned by the family were sought.

In the second part, information was sought on the migration status of the respondents. Information like their place of origin, who was the first one in the family to migrate, when and why did they migrate were sought.

In the third part, information regarding the factors that motivated the respondents or their parents and so on to migrate from their villages to Chandigarh was obtained.

The fourth part dealt with the information regarding the contact of the respondents with their villages and whether they continued to retain and cultivate agricultural land in the village. Information regarding the mode of land cultivation, sale and purchase of land during the last ten years, how was the money used after the sale, and from where the surplus came to buy more land were sought. Information on the extent of dependence on the income from land, visits to the village, and ideas regarding settlement in villages at some stage in life were also collected. An attempt was also made to know whether the respondents wanted their children to maintain the connections with the villages and carry on agriculture.

The fifth part dealt with the notions and changing attitudes of the respondents towards rural and urban life. Information was also sought from the respondents regarding their preference for occupations (ideally) and how would they rank them.

In the next part of interview schedule, the attitudes towards mate selection was sought Information was sought on the respondent views towards approval of their children to marry according to their own choice, age at marriage of girls and boys, give and take of dowry, and qualities ideally preferred in their spouse and gender equality.

In the following section, the respondents were asked to rank their preferred identities in the rural and urban context.

FIELD WORK

Once the respondents were told about the nature of the study, they were quite willing to answer the questions which I asked them. Since all of them were educated, I did not face any problem in communicating with the respondents. Given the nature of the study, only educated and prosperous members of the community were interviewed.

TABULATION AND ANALYSIS OF THE DATA

Although the nature of the study was qualitative, for the convenience of analysis, most of the responses were quantified and tabulated. A code design was prepared, and coding was done in order to prepare the tables.

Some of the qualitative data were catalogued through putting them together according to the subject.

EXPERIENCE AND DIFFICULTIES ENCOUNTERED

It was a very good experience for me to meet all these respondents. Some of them even went to the extent of offering lunch at their place. They were very happy to know that a study was being conducted on them. They all were very willing to answer all the questions and discussed many other informal things regarding their community. Many of them even asked me to send them a copy of the conclusions of my study.

I did face a few problems, especially in taking appointments from the respondents. On an average, an interview took around forty minutes. Some of them were hesitant about giving information regarding their land holdings. Despite these obstacles, the respondents on the whole were very co-operative. The field work proved to be a very enriching experience, and I enjoyed a lot and came to know about many simple facts of the Jat Sikhs in Chandigarh. The field work was completed in approximately ten and a half months' time between May 2000 and July 2001.

CHAPTER 3

JATS IN CHANDIGARH:

THE SOCIO-ECONOMIC BACKGROUND

Jat Sikhs are the main dominant caste in the Punjab countryside. They possess all the attributes of dominance, viz. ownership and control of land, numerical preponderance, relatively high-caste status, reputation for aggression, considerable amount of control over positions of power in Panchayati Raj institutions, co-operatives, land mortgage banks, state legislation, army, police, bureaucracy, etc.

The majority of Jat Sikhs belong to the rural areas of Punjab, and most of them are agriculturalists. With green revolution in the late sixties, a lot of changes have taken place in the Punjab countryside. Punjab became the most prosperous state of the country in terms of per capita income. The large landowning farmers obviously gained more from the green revolution. Many of them were also able to accumulate surpluses.

The socio-economic backgrounds of a particular group of people reveal their places in society. At the same time, these conditions largely depend upon the scope that a particular career offers. This is how we can explain similar class backgrounds of a group in the same occupation. The significance of the background, from the point of view of the sociologist, is that it enables one to study the various factors which are responsible for the status of the individuals in different spheres.

The present study, as mentioned above, was undertaken in order to understand the mobility among the Jat Sikhs of Punjab and the factors that motivated them to migrate to Chandigarh. It also attempts to study their changing notions regarding rural and urban lifestyles.

In the present chapter, an attempt has been made to provide an introduction of the respondents in terms of their socio-economic characteristics such as age, family occupation, socio-economic class, housing status, assets owned by the family in Chandigarh, members staying in the house, number of earning members in the family, numbers students in the family, history of migration, place of origin, and factors that motivated them to migrate to Chandigarh.

AGE OF THE RESPONDENTS

Age is a very important factor that influences all aspects of one's life. One's ideas and attitudes undergo a change with age. Given the nature of the study, younger members of the Jat Sikhs caste in Chandigarh were preferred as respondents (between the age group of 20 and 40 years).

Table 3.1

Age of the Respondents

	Age in Years				
Respondents	20–25	26–30	31–35	36–40	Total
	16	19	16	09	60
	(26.66)	(31.67)	(26.67)	(15.00)	(100)

Note: Percentages are given in parenthesis.

The above table shows that 26.66 per cent of the respondents belonged to the age group of twenty to twenty-five years, 31.67 per cent were in age group of twenty-six to thirty years, 26.67 per cent were in the age group thirty-one to thirty-five years of age, and the remaining 15 per cent of the respondents were in the age group of thirty-six to forty years.

FAMILY OCCUPATION

The respondents could be classified into six different categories with regard to their family occupations. They are as follows

1. Agriculture
2. Agriculture + business
3. Business
4. Ex-Servicemen + Agriculture

5. Government or Private Job
6. Job + agriculture

Table 3.2

Family Occupation of the Respondents

Resp. Agri	Agri + Buss	Buss.	Ex-Def. + Agri	Job	Job +Agri	Total
20	24	03	04	02	07	60
(33.33)	(40.00)	(5.00)	(6.67)	(3.33)	(11.67)	(100)

Note: Percentages are given in parenthesis.

Resp. = Respondent; Agri = Agriculture; Buss = Business; Ex-Def. = Ex-Defence.

The above table shows that 33.33 per cent of the respondents practiced agriculture as the main occupation. Forty per cent of them were those who practiced agriculture as well as had some business in Chandigarh. Only three of the respondents were those who had business as their main source of income. Another 6.67 per cent of the respondents were the ex-servicemen who had agricultural land, that is, they had agriculture and pension as the source of income. Only two of the respondents were engaged in government or private jobs, and another 11.67 per cent had a job plus income from agriculture.

It was relevant that the maximum percentage of migrants still practiced agriculture as their main occupation with some side business in the city. This revealed the importance of land for the Jat Sikhs living in Chandigarh. Even though they had migrated from the rural areas to urban areas, most of them still depended on agriculture as their source of income.

SOCIO-ECONOMIC CLASS

The self-perception of socio-economic class of the respondent tells us about the status and position of migrants in the city. The respondents could be divided into six classes, namely, lower-middle, middle, upper-middle, upper, landlords, and farmers.

Table 3.3

Socio-Economic Class of the Respondents

Resp. Low Mid	Mid.	Upp. Mid	Upp.	Landlords	Farmers	Total
–	7	27	7	19	–	60
–	(11.67)	(45)	(11.67)	(31.66)	–	(100)

Note: Percentages are given in parenthesis.

Low. Mid = Lower-Middle; Upp. Upper

The table shows that 11.67 per cent of the respondents described themselves as belonging to middle class. Another 45 per cent chose to identify themselves as belonging to the upper-middle class and the remaining 11.67 per cent to the upper class. As many as 31.66 per cent of the respondents were the ones who identified themselves as the landlords (none used the vernacular expression zamindar for themselves.). The interesting thing is that none of the respondents identified themselves as belonging to the lower-middle or the farmer class. Even though they had less land, they did not identify themselves as farmers or belonging to lower-middle class families.

NUMBER OF HOUSES OWNED IN PUNJAB

The number of houses owned by the respondents in Punjab also reflects their socio-economic position.

Table 3.4

Number of Houses Owned in Punjab

Resp.	One	Two	None	Total
	24	6	30	60
	(40)	(10)	(50)	(100)

Note: Percentages are given in parenthesis.

As shown in the table half of the respondents had completely migrated to Chandigarh as they reported that they had no other houses elsewhere in the state of Punjab. However, 40 per cent of the respondents owned a house in the state though they were currently living in Chandigarh. Only 10 per cent of the respondents had more than one hous This showed that 50 per cent of the respondents who had migrated from the rural areas still had houses in their native villages. This reflected upon their bonds with their native place. Remaining 50 per cent had land but not the house as they had a house in Chandigarh.

THE TYPE OF RESIDENCE IN CHANDIGARH

The presently occupied place of residence of the respondents was another criterion to know about their socio-economic position. The type of residence could be divided into three categories after the analysis of data. These three categories were

1. Own house
2. Rental
3. Hostel

Table 3.5

Presently Occupied Residence

Resp.	Owned	Rented	Hostel	Total
	43	2	15	60
	(72)	(3.33)	(25.00)	(100)

Note: Percentages are given in parenthesis.

The table indicates that majority of the respondents, that is, 71.66 per cent lived in their own houses in Chandigarh. Only two of the respondents were staying in rented accommodation, and 25 per cent were putting up in the hostels. These 25 per cent of the respondents lived in university halls and were the ones who were here for their further education and thus hoping a better job opportunity in future. This also showed that 72 per cent respondents were not the permanent residents of this city.

MEMBERS STAYING IN THE PRESENT HOUSE

The size of the family reflects the type of the family. Most of the migrants have their families staying with them in Chandigarh which includes their wives and children. Some also have their old parents, unmarried/married brothers and sisters living with them.

Table 3.6

Number of Members Staying in Present House

Resp.	One	Two	Three	Four	More than Four	None	Total
	3	5	14	15	6	17	60
	(5)	(8.33)	(23.33)	(25)	(10)	(28.33)	(100)

Note: Percentages are given in parenthesis.

The table above indicates that only three respondents had one additional member of the family staying in the house, and 8.33 per cent of them had two family members, and 25 per cent had four members in their house. Only a small number of them had more than four family members staying with them (10 per cent). This was not applicable to 28.33 per cent of the respondents as either they were living in university halls or were a newly married couple or brother, sister, or mother and son staying together.

ASSETS OWNED BY THE FAMILY

As mentioned earlier (Chapter 1), those farmers who benefits from the new technology and generated surplus bought Maruti cars and all the consumer goods that signified the lifestyles of the urban middle class.

Therefore, a study of the assets owned by the family in Chandigarh also throws light upon the socio-economic background of the respondents. This also tells us about the needs and demands of the respondents in Chandigarh who had migrated from the small villages.

Table 3.7

Assets Owned by the Family

Assets	In Village (%)	In City (%)	Desirable (%)
Tractor	38 (63.33)	-	3 (5.00)
Car	26 (43.33)	50 (83.33)	05 (8.33)
Motorbike	31 (51.66)	22 (36.66)	02 (3.33)
Dish Antenna	26 (43.33)	08 (13.33)	02 (3.33)
VCR	15 (25.00)	40 (66.66)	05 (8.33)
T.V.	38 (63.33)	44 (73.33)	01 (1.66)
Video Camera	06 (10.00)	25 (41.66)	12 (20.00)
A.C.	19 (31.66)	38 (68.33)	09 (15.00)
Washing Machine	25 (41.66)	41 (68.33)	06 (10.00)
Microwave Oven	03 (5.00)	36 (60.00)	09 (15.00)
Fridge	32 (53.33)	51 (85.00)	01 (1.66)
Cooking Gas	32 (53.33)	50 (83.33)	01 (1.66)
CD-Player	24 (40.00)	42 (70.00)	07 (11.66)

The table above shows that the 83.33 per cent, that is, a majority of the respondents owned a car, and 8.33 desired to have one. Motorbike was owned by 36.66 per cent and only two of them desired to buy it. Another 13.33 per cent of the respondents owned their dish antennas and rest all had cable connections. Video cassette recorder was owned by 66.66 per cent of the respondents. Another 73.33 per cent of the respondents had televisions, and the remaining who did not have a care were the once studying at university. Video camera was possessed by 41.66 per cent of the respondents, and 20 per cent desired to own it. As much as 63.33 per cent had air-conditioner at their residence and 15 per cent of the respondents desired to have it. Washing machine was used by 68.33 per cent of the respondents, and 10 per cent of the respondents desired but it. Another 60 per cent of the respondents had a microwave oven, and 15 per cent were planning to buy it. Majority of the respondents, that is, 85 per cent had a fridge. Cooking gas was owned by 83.33 per cent of the respondents. Almost a majority, that is 70 per cent of the respondents owned a CD-player, and the remaining 11.66 desired to have one.

EARNING MEMBERS IN THE FAMILY

Living in a city is expensive, and in order to make both ends meet, more than one member of the family have to earn and supplement the household income. Therefore, it was necessary to know about the members who earned in the family. This was important in order to get the information regarding the socio-economic position of the respondents.

Table 3.8

Earning Members in the Family

Resp.	One	Two	Three	Four	All Members	NA	Total
	23	4	4	1	14	14	60
	(38.33)	(6.66)	(6.66)	(1.66)	(23.33)	(23.33)	100

Note: Percentages are given in parenthesis.

NA = Not applicable

The table above indicates that 38.33 per cent of the respondent families had just one earning head and 6.66 per cent of the families had atleast two earning members. A small per cent of, that is, 6.66, respondents had at least three earning heads, and only one respondent had four members in the family who earned. Another 23.33 per cent of the migrant families were such who had all the members working and earning. But this was not applicable to 23.33 per cent of the respondents as they were still students. This showed that with the time and demands to be fulfilled; most of the grown-up members of the family had to earn in order to live a comfortable life in a city.

NUMBER OF STUDENTS IN THE FAMILY

Many respondents had migrated to Chandigarh for the purpose of further studies or for the reason of better education in the schools and colleges available here for their children. Therefore, it was important to know about the number of students in the families as education was one of the major factors behind their migration from rural to urban areas.

Table 3.9

Number of Students in the Family

Resp.	One	Two	Three	None	NA	Total
	14	18	1	13	14	60
	(23.33)	(30)	(1.66)	(21.66)	(23.33)	(100)

Note: Percentages are given in parenthesis.

The table above showed that 23.33 per cent of the respondents had only one student in their family, while 30 per cent had two members as regular students. Only one respondent had three students, and 21.66 per cent of the respondents did not have any student in their family because either they were a newly married couple or a mother and son or brother and sister living together. Remaining 23.33 per cent of the respondents were students themselves who had come to Chandigarh for their higher education.

THE HISTORY OF MIGRATION

Sorokin's work is regarded as the pioneering study in 'social mobility'. According to him, 'social mobility is understood by any transition of an individual or social object, or value from one social position to another' (Sorokin, 1959).

According to Peterson (1970), the migration will be conservative if the migrants settle down at new places but continue with the land-related activities. However, it will be innovative if the people uprooted from rural or urban areas alike work for capitalist enterprises such as modern factories (Petersen, 1970).

As this study was aimed to study the pattern of mobility among the Jat Sikhs of Punjab, it was important to know about the first person from the family of these respondents to migrate to Chandigarh. It was important to know which generation of the respondents migrated to Chandigarh first.

Table 3.10

History of Migration

Resp.	Father	Self	Mother	Grandfather	Total
	15	38	3	4	60
	(25.00)	(63.33)	(5)	(6.66)	(100)

Note: Percentages are given in parenthesis.

The table above indicates that in case of 25 per cent of the respondents, their father was the first person to come and settle down in Chandigarh. A large majority, that is, 63.33 per cent of the respondents were themselves the first one's who came and settled in Chandigarh permanently or temporarily. Only three of the respondents came with their mother and another four of them informed that their grandparents were the first ones to migrate to Chandigarh. Thus, they were the third generation living in the city and settled down here.

THE AREA OF MIGRATION FROM PUNJAB

The region from which these respondents had migrated to Chandigarh was also an important part of our study. An attempt was made to know about the areas from where maximum number of people had come and settled down in Chandigarh.

Table 3.11

The Area of Migration from Punjab

Resp.	Malwa	Majha	Doaba	No. Res.	Raj, Hyr.	Total
	37	5	6	8	4	60
	(61.66)	(8.33)	(10)	(13.33)	(6.66)	(100)

Note: Percentages are given in parenthesis.

No Res = No Response; Raj = Rajasthan; Hyr = Haryana.

The table indicates that 61.66 per cent, which was the majority of the respondents, were from the Malwa region of Punjab. Another 8.33 were from Majha region, and 10 per cent were from Doaba region of Punjab. Remaining 13.33 per cent of the migrants gave no response and said that they were the natives of Chandigarh. Only four of the respondents were from Rajasthan and Haryana.

TYPE OF MIGRATION

After knowing about the region from where these respondents had migrated, the type of migration becomes important. For this study, three types of migration categories were taken into consideration:

1. Permanent
2. Temporary
3. Students

Table 3.12

Types of Migration

Resp.	Permanent	Temporary	Students	Total
	40	5	15	60
	(66.66)	(8.33)	(25.00)	(100)

Note: Percentages are given in parenthesis.

The table shows that 66.66 per cent of the respondents were the ones who had permanently settled in Chandigarh, and 8.33 had migrated to Chandigarh on temporary basis, and 25 per cent were the students who had come to Chandigarh to further pursue their studies and career. Thus, a majority of the respondents settled down in this city on permanent basis.

MOTIVATING FACTORS FOR MIGRATION TO CHANDIGARH

A multiple of factors had motivated them to migrate from rural areas of Punjab to Chandigarh. The following table shows the number of factors these respondents mentioned for their moving to Chandigarh.

Table 3.13

Motivating Factors for Migration to Chandigarh

Sr. No.	Factors	Resp (%)
1.	Higher Education/Children's Education	23 (38.33)
2.	Job Opp./Employed/Business/High Court	5 (8.33)
3.	New City Developed/Modern easy lifestyle/Retired from Job	4 (6.66)
4.	Job/Education/Business/City life easy and modern	5 (25.00)
5.	Terrorism/Riots	1 (1.66)
6.	Got Married	15 (25.00)
7.	No Particular Reason/Had a House in city thus migrated	2 (3.33)

The table indicates that 38.33 per cent of the respondents had come to Chandigarh either for their own higher education or for the education of their children. Another 8.33 per cent were employed here in Chandigarh, or they had their own business or legal practice in high court. Only four of them said that Chandigarh was a new modern city or where parents settled here after retirement because of the modern amenities that Chandigarh offered.

A good per cent of respondents, that is, twenty-five of the respondents had come to Chandigarh either for a job or for education or for business and the city's modern easy lifestyle. Just one of the respondents gave terrorism or riots as the reason for coming to Chandigarh. Twenty-five per cent of the migrants got married and thus were settled in Chandigarh (all were female respondents). Only two of them had no particular reason to migrate and settle down in this city, or they had a house in Chandigarh and so they migrated to Chandigarh just like that.

After having discussed the socio-economic background of the respondents, the following chapter presents data on the linkages that the migrant Jat Sikhs in Chandigarh continue to have with their native village.

CHAPTER 4

JATS IN CHANDIGARH: THE RURAL LINKAGES

This chapter focuses on the links maintained by the Jat Sikhs migrants with their rural base and the nature of these links. It also aims to analyse whether these migrants depend on land for social prestige, income, grains, assets, ready cash through tenancy, sale for construction of house or business investment, and purchase of consumer goods.

Connell (et.al. 1976) has mentioned that a certain minimum level of income is necessary before migration can take place. It is the members of relatively large landowning families in the villages who can best afford the costs, risks, and delayed returns associated with migration. The distance of migration reflects the cost of the migration process. This cost in terms of forgone earnings and increased cost of living is a vital component of migration. The initial costs of fares, residence in town, the purchase of consumables, etc. has to be met after migration. A migrant runs the risk of not finding a particular job or attaining a particular status which he aspired for. Thus, only those individuals who can afford to take risks and bear the cost of migration migrate voluntarily.

The large landowners possess money to finance their migration. Their migration to the city is not only voluntary but also motivated by an aspiration for upward social mobility of the family.

The financial costs of moving are generally high, and in order to meet these costs, many landowners (with medium and small landholdings) do not mind selling their lands. Thus, with sufficient capital at hand, they can afford the risks and costs associated with migration. On the other hand, many small farmers or landholders sell their land in order to invest that money in business in a city or urban property as they do not find agriculture to be rewarded enough.

One of the aims of this study was to find out the changing attitudes of Jat Sikhs towards rural lifestyle and their notions of rurality. The respondents were asked to tell five positive and negative things regarding rural life and whether they wanted their children to keep the village connections alive and carry on agriculture. The data presented below also shows whether they have sold or bought agricultural land in last ten years, how was the surplus money used, from where the money came for the purchase of additional land, how was the money invested, to what extent were these respondents dependent upon the income from land, how often did they go to their village, and whether they had any plans of returning to the village.

ACRES OF AGRICULTURAL LAND IN VILLAGE

According to Kaur (1986), 'For Jats, it seems that there is an equal emphasis on the Jat (caste) part of the identity and also on the Zamindar part of it. The latter emphasizes both occupation and ownership of land. The Jat might be employed as a school teacher, or serve in the military but he sees his primary role as that of an agriculturist. This connection with land is what he holds most dear and what identifies him.'

Table 4.1

Acres of Agricultural Land Owned

Resp.	<2.5	2.5–5	5–10	10–25	25–50	50–100	100 and above	NA	Total
	Marginal	Small	Middle	Big					
	–	1	7	19	13	13	6	1	60
	–	(1.66)	(11.66)	(31.66)	(21.66)	(21.66)	(10)	(1.66)	(100)

Note: Percentages are given in parenthesis.

The table indicates that only one of the respondents had a small land holding, that is, between 2.5 and 5 acres of land, and none of the respondents were the marginal farmers, that is, up to or less than 2.5 acres of land. Another 11.66 per cent were the middle landowners having agricultural land between 5 and 10 acres, and 31.66 per cent were the big land owners, having land between 10 and 25 acres. Another 21.66 per cent had 25 to 50 acres of agricultural land and almost the same per cent of the respondents had 50 to 100, that is, surplus land holdings.

The remaining 10 per cent of the respondents had 100 or above 100 acres of agricultural land. Only one of the respondent did not own any agricultural land in the village as it was sold long time back by his parents.

HOUSE OWNED IN THE VILLAGE

After getting the information about the agricultural land owned by the respondents, it would be useful to know whether they owned a house in the village or not.

Table 4.2

House Owned in the Village

Resp.	Yes	No	Total
	54	6	60
	(90.33)	(10.66)	(100)

Note: Percentages are given in parenthesis.

The table indicates that maximum number of respondents, that is, 90.33 per cent still had a house in the village from where they had migrated, and a very small percentage, that is, 10.66 per cent did not have a house in the village any more. Either they had sold off all the agricultural land and had no links with the village now or they had very small landholdings.

MODES OF CULTIVATION OF LAND

There was a tendency among large and medium landowners to lease out their land after migration to the city.

Balgopal (1987) has described a typical family of the agricultural capitalist class as the one that 'has a landownings in its natural village cultivated by hired labour, bataidar, tenant or arm servants and supervised by the father or one son, business of various description in own managed by other sons and perhaps a young and bright child who is a doctor, engineer or a professor' (Balgopal, 1987).

The table below shows the type of cultivation practiced by the respondents.

Table 4.3

Mode of Cultivation of Land

Resp.	Other Members of the Family	Leased Out on Share	Leased Out on Cash	Farm Servants	Leased Cash + Family	NA	Total
	23	1	20	10	5	1	60
	(38.33)	(1.66)	(33.33)	(16.66)	(8.33)	(1.66)	(100)

Note: Percentages are given in parenthesis.

The table shows that 38.33 per cent of the respondents had other family members looking after their farms. Only one of the respondents managed his farms by giving them on lease on share basis, and 33.33 per cent had leased out their farms on annual cash contract. The table also indicates that 16.66 per cent of them had given their farms in the hands of trustworthy servants. The remaining 8.33 per cent of the respondents had leased out some part of their land, and the rest of the land was looked after by the other family members. This was not applicable to one respondent as he no more owned agricultural land in the village.

AGRICULTURAL LAND SOLD IN LAST TEN YEARS

The table below reflects that agricultural land continued to be of crucial importance to Jats even when they had migrated to the urban areas. Most of them continued to practice agriculture as one of their main occupations. It was not easy for them to part away from their land.

Therefore, selling off the land was not very common among them.

Table 4.4

Agricultural Land Sold in Last Ten Years

Resp.	Yes	No	NA	Total
	17	42	1	60
	(28.33)	(70)	(1.66)	(100)

Note: Percentages are given in parenthesis.

The table indicates that 28.33 per cent of the respondents had sold out some land, and the majority of the respondents had not sold out any agricultural land in the last ten years.

Table 4.5

Agricultural Land Bought in Last Ten Years

Resp.	Yes	No	Total
	17	43	60
	(28.33)	(71.66)	(100)

Note: Percentages are given in parenthesis.

On the contrary, as shown in the above table, as many as 28.33 per cent of the respondents had in fact bought land in last ten years. However, a majority of the respondents had not bought any agricultural land during last ten years as mentioned above.

When these respondents were asked to mention the source of income to buy more agricultural land, they offered following responses.

Table 4.6

Source to Buy More Land

Resp.	Business/ Agriculture	Land Sold	Land Property	Job Professional	NA	Total
	7	6	1	3	43	60
	(11.66)	(10)	(1.66)	(5)	(71.66)	(100)

Note: Percentages are given in parenthesis.

The table indicates that 11.66 per cent of the respondents got the surplus money to buy more land from their business and agriculture. Another 10 per cent had sold their high-valued agricultural land and reinvested the money in purchase of cheaper land. Only one of the respondents had sold some other property and bought agricultural land with that money. While another three of them got the money from their jobs or professions. This was not applicable to a majority of the respondents as they had not bought agricultural land in last ten years.

How was the money invested by those who had sold agricultural land?

Table 4.7

Money Invested in After Selling Land

Resp.	Business	Land	Property	Land/Property/ Business	NA	Total
	5	5	5	1	44	60
	(8.33)	(8.33)	(8.33)	(1.66)	(73.33)	(100)

Note: Percentages are given in parenthesis.

The table indicates that 8.33 per cent of the respondents invested the surplus money in their business. Another 8.33 per cent had bought agricultural land elsewhere. Some others had invested the amount in the purchase of property except land (8.33 per cent). Only one of them had invested the money in land or business or property. This was not applicable to the majority of the respondents as they did not sell any agricultural land during the last ten years.

NUMBER OF ACRES OF LAND SOLD (DURING LAST TEN YEARS)

As mentioned earlier, it was not easy for the Jats to part away from their land. So, even when they were forced to sell off their land, they sold it out in parts and not wholly. It became important to know about the acres of land sold by the respondents in last ten years.

Table 4.8

Number of Acres of Land Sold in Last Ten Years

Resp.	<5	5–10	10-15	15–20	20 and Above	NA	Total
	6	4	4	1	1	44	60
	(10)	(6.66)	(6.66)	(1.66)	(1.66)	(73.33)	(100)

Note: Percentages are given in parenthesis.

The table shows that 10 per cent of the respondents had sold less than 5 acres of land. Another four of them had sold 5 to 10 acres, and an equal per cent of the respondents had sold land between 10 and 15 acres. Only one of the respondents had sold 15 to 20 acres of land, and another one had sold land between 20 and more acres. 44 respondents had not sold any agricultural land in last ten years.

NUMBER OF ACRES OF LAND BOUGHT (DURING LAST TEN YEARS)

Of the sixty respondents interviewed for the study, as many as seventeen reported to have purchased additional agricultural land during the last ten years. The table below indicates that 8.33 per cent of the respondents bought less than 5 acres of land, and 10 per cent of the respondents bought more land between 5 and 10 acres. While two of the respondents bought land between 10 and 15 acres, and only one respondent bought land between 15 and 20 acres. In the category of twenty and above acres, only three respondents were there, and this was not applicable for a majority of the respondents as they did not buy any agricultural land during the last ten years.

Table 4.9

Number of Acres of Land Bought in Last Ten Years

Resp.	<5	5–10	10-15	15–20	20 and Above	NA	Total
	5	6	2	1	3	43	60
	(8.33)	(10)	(3.33)	(1.66)	(5)	(71.66)	(100)

Note: Percentages are given in parenthesis.

EXTENT OF DEPENDENCE ON INCOME FROM LAND

The following tells us about how far the respondents and their families continued to depend upon the income from agriculture.

Table 4.10

Dependence on Income from Land

	Entirely	Mostly	Marginally	Hardly	N.A.	Total
Resp.	15	14	21	9	1	60
	(25.00)	(23.33)	(35.00)	(15.00)	(1.66)	(100)

Note: Percentages are given in parenthesis.

The table indicates that 25 per cent of the respondents reported that they were entirely dependent upon the income from land. Another 23.33 per cent were the ones who mostly depended upon the income from the agricultural land, and 35 per cent of the respondents marginally depended upon their land for income. Another nine of the respondents hardly depended on the income from land, and only one of them reported that they did not depend on land at all.

CONTACT WITH THE VILLAGE

Regarding the nature of ties between the respondents and their native village, Joshi (1994) stated that the rural population was too strongly tied to its village of origin by bonds of kinship, marriage, customs, land, and cultures of in group living. He has also concluded that migrants maintained a close contact with their native places through visits and remittances (Joshi, 1994; p.34).

Joshi (1994) also pointed about the migrant's frequency of visits to their villages in order to maintain ties and solidarity with their extended families (Joshi, 1994; p.105).

Sir Malcolm Darling talks about the Punjabi Jat Sikh migrant and remarks,

'A vigorous climate and healthy diet nurture the kind of enterprise which will actively search for a solution to such problem the sturdy peasant will seek a supplement or an alternative in the army, in the canal colonies or overseas. Eventually he will return to his village with funds sufficient to purchase what his inheritance had failed to bestow on him.' This trend of return may not be there anymore, but it throws light on the kind of relationship the Jat Sikh traditionally shared with their land' (c.f. Barrier and Duisenberg 1989: 350).

Table 4.11

Visits to the Village

	Weekly	Fortnightly	Monthly	Whenever Possible	Never Visited	N.A.	Total
Resp.	6	8	13	31	1	1	60
	(10)	(13.33)	(21.66)	(51.66)	(1.66)	(1.66)	(100)

The table indicates that 10 per cent of the respondents visited their villages once in a week and another 13.33 per cent in a fortnight. Remaining 21.66 per cent of the respondents visited their villages monthly, and more than half of the respondents visited their village whenever it was possible for them to go. Only one of the respondent said that he had never visited a village in his whole life, and this was not applicable to one of them as he no more had agricultural land.

SETTLING DOWN IN THE VILLAGE

As these respondents had maintained relations with their land and village, it becomes important to know whether they would go back and settle down in the village at any stage of their life or not.

Table 4.12

Settling Down in the Village

Resp.	Yes	No	May Be	Total
	20	37	3	60
	(33.33)	(61.66)	(5.00)	(100)

Note: Percentages are given in parenthesis.

The table indicates that 33.33 per cent of the respondents wanted to go and settle down in the village, and a majority of them did not want to settle down in the village at any stage in their life.

Only three of them were not sure, and they might settle in village but at a later stage in their life.

When these respondents were asked whether they would like their children to keep the village connections alive and maintain relationships with their village, they gave the following responses.

Table 4.13

Children to Maintain the Village Connections Alive

Resp.	Yes	No	May Be	Depends on Them	Total
	37	9	9	5	60
	(61.66)	(15)	(15)	(8.33)	(100)

Note: Percentages are given in parenthesis.

A majority of the respondents wanted their children to keep their village connections alive. Another nine of them did not want their children to have any links with their village or land, and again nine of them were not sure of themselves in this regard. Rest 8.33 per cent of the respondents said that they would leave it on their children to decide.

The respondents were also asked to tell whether they wanted their children to carry on with agriculture.

Table 4.14

Children to Carry on Agriculture

Resp.	Yes	No	May Be	Depends on Them	As a Side Business	Total
	28	14	2	6	10	60
	(46.66)	(23.33)	(3.33)	(10)	(16.66)	(100)

Note: Percentages are given in parenthesis.

The table indicates that 46.66 per cent of the respondents wanted their children to carry on with agriculture as a main occupation. Another 23.33 per cent did not want this. Only two of the respondents were not sure of what they wanted, and 10 per cent left it out on their children to decide. The remaining 16.66 per cent of the respondents wanted their children to practice agriculture but as a side business only.

NOTIONS OF RURALITY

As the respondents had left their native rural land and settled in Chandigarh, it became important to know what they felt about the life in the village. An attempt was made to know about the positive qualities of the rural life. The reasons why these respondents visited their native villages and what were the good characteristics of the village life became significant with regard to their notions of rurality. The respondents were asked to give five positive features of rural life.

Table 4.15

Positive Qualities of Rural Life

Qualities/Reasons	Response (Percentage)
Parents and relatives there/friendly, simple, honest, and helpful people.	40 (66.66)
Good environment/healthy food.	49 (81.66)
Simple lifestyles/enjoyment and recreation/ no stress and tensions of city life/less expensive, and change from city life.	35 (58.33)
Close to their roots/culture/they belong to that place, good for upbringing of children.	20 (33.33)
High status there/indentify themselves with rural life/upper castes/bossy.	12 (20.00)
All facilities available/no problems in the villages nowadays.	5 (8.33)
No positive point.	2 (3.33)

The table indicates that a majority of the respondents said that they liked the village life because their parents and relatives still lived in the villages. The village people were simple, friendly, and honest. Good environment, healthy food, close to the nature, and pollution-free atmosphere are some of the good qualities mentioned by 81.66 per cent of the respondents. More than half, that is, 58.33 per cent, of the respondents agreed that villages had simple lifestyles, free from modern life stresses and tensions of city life. They enjoyed visiting their native village as it was a change from city life, and living in the village was less expensive as compared to the city. Another 33.33 per cent of the respondent felt close to their roots and culture when they were in their village. They had a sense of belongingness, and it was good for the upbringing of their children. There were twelve respondents who identified with the village life because it offered them high status as they belonged to the upper caste in the village. Some of them also said that the villages of Punjab had all the amenities of urban living and thus life in village was as comfortable as in the town. Only two of the respondents did not have any positive quality in the village lifestyle.

NEGATIVE QUALITIES OF RURAL LIFE

After knowing the positive qualities about the rural life, respondents were asked to identify some negative qualities of the rural life.

Table 4.16

Negative Qualities of Rural Life

Qualities/Reasons	Response (Percentage)
Basic amenities not available	42 (70.00)
Politics/casteism/No awareness	14 (23.33)
Limited social life/less recreation	15 (25.00)
Narrow-minded people/Interference of relatives/gossip	17 (28.33)
Less progress/stagnant/no work/more prone to addiction (alcohol, etc.)	17 (28.33)
Standard of living is low/poor people	3 (5.00)
Family feuds/fights/jealousy	5 (8.33)
More distance from Chandigarh	2 (3.33)
Women are ill-treated/not free	3 (5.00)
No negative point/enjoy being there/stay for few days.	6 (10.00)

The table indicates that a majority of the respondents agreed to the fact that the basic amenities of life were not available in the rural areas. Politics, castesim, and lack of awareness were other weak points given by 23.33 per cent of the respondents. Another 25 per cent respondents stated that rural life had limited opportunities for social interaction and less amount of recreation. Narrow-mindedness, gossip, and interference of the relatives were mentioned by 28.33 per cent of the respondents as being negative features of the rural life. Another reason that the village life was stagnant, less progressive, more prone to addiction was given by 28.33 per cent respondents. Only three of the respondents mentioned that village people had a low standard of living and were poor. Another five of them said that family feuds and jealousy were very common among the villagers. Only two of the respondents informed that the negative quality of their village was that it was far away from Chandigarh. Another three respondents agreed that women had a low status, were illiterate, and were not free to do anything according to their own wishes in the rural areas. The remaining 10 per cent respondents enjoyed themselves in village as they visited the village for a few days only and found no negative point in the village life.

Thus, we can say that in spite of the migration to Chandigarh, the Jats are closely linked with their land and maintain strong ties with their villages. A good number of them even wanted to settle down in villages at some later stage in their life. They also wanted their children to maintain links with their village life and carry on agriculture, thus keeping ties with the land alive.

CHAPTER 5
JATS IN CHANDIGARH: CHANGING LIFESTYLES AND IDENTITY

Davis (1965) has defined urbanisation on the basis of demographic change, viz, immigration to the urban centres and concentration of migrants in a few cities. According to Lewis (1965), urbanisation is 'not a single, unitary, universally similar process but assumes different forms and meanings depending upon the prevailing historic, economic, social and cultural conditions' (Lewis, 1965; 495).

Wirth (1939) developed a minimum sociological definition of city 'as a relatively large, dense and permanent settlement of socially heterogeneous individuals.' According to his proposition, the increase in the number, density, and heterogeneity of population led to the emergence of a society in which the nature of relationships was transformed from personal and primary to the secondary contacts, offer transitory, formal, and impersonal (Wirth, 1939; p.7).

Being an agriculturally developed region, the pattern of urbanisation in Punjab has understandingly been different from the classical patterns of urbanisation. Due to agrarian prosperity, industrialisation has not been the only source of urbanisation in Punjab.

After green revolution, urbanisation took place in Punjab. There was spurt in the process of urbanisation and of agricultural marketing cum trading towns in particular as a consequence of the agricultural surplus. This also provided a stimulus for urban marketing and trade. The rapid agricultural growth also led to a greater degree of occupational diversification in the state. Though industrialisation remains the main motivating force for urbanisation, at the same time, the state is dominated by a larger number of small and medium towns which specialise in trade, marketing processing of agricultural produce, provision of agricultural implements, etc. However one can also observe a tendency for the concentration of population in the class I cities due to spatial inequality in the pattern of industrialisation and other factors pulling towards the big cities, thus affecting the balanced returns of urbanisation previously seen in Punjab.

The agricultural prosperity also led to emergence of a new class of farmers that had accumulated enough resources to go beyond the village and seek greener pastures in the towns. According to Gill (1994), the migration from rural to urban areas in the subsequent three decades of 1961–71, 1971–81, and 1981–91 was, respectively, 15.75 per cent, 49.13 per cent, and 30.32 per cent (Gill, 1994).

A large majority of the landowning population of Punjab belongs to a particular caste, viz, Jats. The rural to urban mobility of this type is largely confined to the big Jat farmers. The process of migration and urbanisation obviously led to many changes in the lifestyles of the migrants.

According to Gerth and Mills (1958), 'the terms life styles is used interchangeably with "styles of life" in the sociological literature. It was Max Weber who first used the term "style of life" to indicate consumption patterns.' Poter (1965) too viewed 'style of life' as being related to consumption pattern. According to Mayer and Buckley (1970), 'it is a status group which is characterized by specific behavioral patterns which may be designed as a style of life.'

Thus, one can see that with urbanisation many changes were likely in the lifestyles of the Jats who had migrated from the rural areas to Chandigarh and experienced horizontal and vertical mobility. This chapter attempts to look at the process of urbanisation among the Jats Sikhs and their changing life styles and identity.

Once the migrants settled down in the city, they obviously start adopting the urban lifestyles. How far the process of urbanisation did have an effect on them with regard to the question of identity? Kaur (1986) in her paper on the Jat Sikhs' identity in rural Punjab observed that 'while at the village level, the Jat did not feel a threat to their identity but beyond village, especially at the regional and national level their concerns became the same as those of urban Sikhs'. She further stated that 'within the village, the Jat is confident of his identity as a Sikh he does not need to declare it by unshorn hair or beard or by participating in Gurudwara activities. However, whenever the Jat farmer goes outside the village, he dons his turban (Kaur, 1986).

Rayaprol (1997) in her book has mentioned that 'for the migrants identities and cultures get delocalized, but they rarely get detached from the memories of past places and times.' Referring to the phenomenon of ethnic identities in the Indian context, Punekar (1947) had identified 'caste, language, region and religion as the four major premises where ethnicity operates in a significant way.'

One of the most important factors responsible for the migration of the respondents from the rural to urban areas is education, that is, education either for self or for the children. So it becomes important to know about the educational qualifications of the respondents.

Table 5.1

Educational Qualification (Respondent)

Resp.	Graduate	PG	Professional (Dr, Engg., IAS, Law, MBA, Ph.D etc)	Total
	25	20	15	60
	(41.66)	(33.33)	(25.00)	(100)

Note: Percentages are given in parenthesis.

The table indicates that 41.66 per cent respondents were graduates. While 33.33 per cent were those who were postgraduates, the remaining 25 per cent were the professionals. These professionals included the doctors, engineers, lawyers, and masters of business management.

After getting the information regarding the educational qualifications, it was necessary to know about the number of years of stay of the respondents in Chandigarh after the migration.

Table 5.2

Number of Years in Chandigarh

Resp.	<5	5–10	11–15	16–20	20 and Above	Total
	8	20	7	6	19	60
	(13.33)	(33.33)	(11.66)	(10)	(31.66)	(100)

Note: Percentages are given in parenthesis.

The table shows that eight of the respondents were the ones who were in Chandigarh for less than five years. Thirty-three per cent of the respondents had been staying in this city for last five to ten years, and seven of them were staying in Chandigarh from last eleven to fifteen years. Ten per cent of respondents came in the group of sixteen to twenty years and the remaining 31.66 per cent respondents had been staying in Chandigarh for twenty and more years.

PREFERENCE FOR OCCUPATION (SELF)

As stated earlier, Jat Sikhs are an agriculturalist caste, concentrated primarily in the rural areas of Punjab. Their other occupation was they joined army as they had a tradition of serving the nation, hence a popular assumption about Jats in relation to their choice of occupation stands. Their first preference was agriculture. It was not only an occupation but a source of pride and identity for them.

Armed forces as mentioned above came next and then the professions like medicine, engineering, computer, teaching, and management. Jats were supposed to dislike the business class and labourers. As stated by one of the respondents, 'Jats could not compete with the business-minded "Banias" or "Lalas" of the city as they did not belong to such occupational backgrounds. Therefore, it was really difficult for them to look for an occupation except agriculture. Even getting business management degrees from abroad, they were not able to compete in business in the cities.'

However, over the years, their attitude towards urban life has been changing. As it has been pointed out by Jodhka (1999), 'those farmers, who benefited from green-revolution in Punjab, did not wish their future generations to continue working as agriculturalist.' He further argued that 'the recent crisis of agriculture and spurt of suicides by farmers in Punjab has taken away the charm that agriculture enjoyed in Punjabi culture. It is not surprising therefore that in Punjab today no one celebrates agriculture. Therefore, people have started moving from rural to urban areas in search of new middle class occupations' (Jodhka, 1999).

Thus, it was thought to be important to know about the occupational preferences of the Jat Sikhs in Chandigarh.

Table 5.3

Preference for Occupation for Self (Ideally)

Occupations	First (%)	Second (%)	Third (%)	Fourth (%)	Fifth (%)
Agriculture	4 (6.66)	16 (26.66)	11 (18.33)	9 (15)	2 (3.33)
Business in City	15 (25)	11 (18.33)	15 (25)	4 (6.66)	8 (13.33)
Profession (Dr, Engg., Research Technology	13 (21.66)	4 (6.66)	7 (11.66)	5 (8.33)	6 (10)
Armed Forces	4 (6.66)	7 (11.66)	3 (5)	8 (13.33)	11 (18.33)
Legal Profession	3 (5)	4 (6.66)	4 (6.66)	5 (8.33)	12 20)
Bureaucracy (IAS, IPS, etc.)	8 (13.33)	10 (16.66)	11 (18.33)	11 (18.33)	2 (3.33)
Computers/ Business	–	7 (11.66)	8 (13.33)	12 (20)	4 (6.66)
Management/ Politics	5 (8.33)	1 (1.66)	–	–	1 (1.66)

The table clearly indicates the preference for the occupations given by the respondent. But to make the data simpler, the first three preferences were clubbed together. High, middle, and low-preferred occupations were then found out. It was found that business in town was the highly preferred occupation as a majority of the respondents preferred this occupation on top. Agriculture followed, and bureaucracy was placed third on the preference table. In the middle category, professions like medicine engineering, research, and technology were there (40 per cent). Then followed computers and management courses (25 per cent).

The low-preferred occupations consist of armed forces, legal profession, and politics.

NOTIONS OF URBANITY

As the migration was from rural to urban area, it was significant to know about the positive and negative qualities of urban life in Chandigarh. This would also reflect upon the changing lifestyles, attitudes, and identities of the respondents in Chandigarh.

Table 5.4

Positive Qualities of Urban Life

Qualities/Reasons	Response (Percentage)
Basic amenities available/good lifestyle	49 (81.66)
Broad-minded people/good social circle	22 (36.66)
Progressive Business/Jobs/exposure to new things/more money/more opportunities.	17 (28.33)
Challenging life/development of personality/ increases the intellect and reasoning	11 (18.33)
Freedom for women	3 (5.00)
Small nuclear families/less interference of relatives	5 (8.33)
Near Shimla	4 (6.66)
Less expensive as compared to other cities/better than other cities	5 (8.33)
Home/born and brought up	5 (8.33)

The table indicates the positive qualities of city as mentioned by the respondents and why they preferred to stay in Chandigarh. It shows that a majority of the respondents agreed that all the basic amenities of life were available in Chandigarh. People had a good lifestyle and enjoyed staying in a city. Whereas 36.66 per cent respondents reported that the city people were broad-minded and they had a good social circle in the city.

Another 28.33 per cent respondents agreed that cities had progressive business, job opportunities were more, exposure to new things was there, and more money could be made while in a city. Another 18.33 per cent found city life more challenging and stated proper development of the personality could take place in a city. It also increased the intellect and reasoning power of the respondents. Only three respondents mentioned that women had freedom in cities.

While five of them preferred city life because they had nuclear families and less interference of the relatives. A few of the respondents preferred to stay in Chandigarh as it was close to the hills and they could go to Shimla whenever they wanted to. Only five of the respondents found Chandigarh to be less expensive and having better environment than other big cities. The remaining five of them liked staying in Chandigarh as this was their home town because they were born and brought up here.

Table 5.5

Negative Qualities of Urban Life

Qualities/Reasons	Response (Percentage)
Diplomacy/show off/status quo/unfriendly people Self-centred/rate race/jealousy/ money-minded people	31 (51.66)
Expensive City	25 (41.66)
Over Populated/slums/more traffic/ pollution/housing problem	27 (45.00)
Lack of morality/media/exposure is corrupting/youth imitating the west	9 (15.00)
Small city/less jobs/people are less career-oriented/slow life/limited business	6 (10.00)
Same feudalistic culture/interference of people	4 (6.66)
Hectic life/tensions/not safe as crime rate is increasing	5 (8.33)
More distance from the village/small families	2 (3.33)
Full of Bureaucrats/power game	9 (15.00)
No. negative point	8 (13.33)

The table above shows the negative points of life in Chandigarh as pointed out by the respondents. More than half of the respondents said that the biggest drawback of living in a city was that people were unfriendly and had diplomatic behaviour. They were self-centred and believed in status quo and rat race. Most of the population of cities consisted of money-minded people, and they were generally jealous of each other. A good per cent, that is, 41.66 of the respondents found Chandigarh an expensive city. Overpopulated, slums, traffic, pollution, and housing problem were mentioned by some of them. Nine of them said that city life lacked morality as the media exposure was corrupting. Youngsters were but imitating the west and led an aimless life. Six of the respondents reported that Chandigarh was a small city with less job and people were less career-oriented. It was marked by slow life, and business was limited in this city. A small number of the respondents said that Chandigarh had the same feudalistic culture like in the villages. People interfered too much in each other's lives. Another five of them said that it was no more a safe city as crime rate was increasing day by day. Life was very hectic and full of tensions. Only two of them were of the view that Chandigarh was far away from their village and thus they had to have nuclear families in the city. Fifteen per cent respondents were of their view that bureaucracy and power game was also one of the negative qualities of life in a city. However, eight of them did not find any negative quality in urban lifestyle.

Traditionally, marriages were settled by the parents and guardians, as a relationship between a husband and a wife. On the contrary, it was a relationship between two families. According to Ross (1987), 'in the Indian culture marriage contract was looked as an agreement between two families rather than two young people.' Mainly due to this reason, it was the responsibility of the family and not the persons concerned to arrange marriage.

However, with the education, growing awareness, media exposure, satellite TV, changes in the lifestyles and attitudes, there is a growing feeling of selecting one's own mate and marrying out of one's own choice.

Table 5.6

Children to Marry According to Their Wishes

Resp.	Yes	No	Not for Girls	Acc. To Family /Caste	Total
Male	14	10	2	4	30
	(46.66)	(33.33)	(6.66)	(13.33)	(100)
Female	18	7	-	5	30
	(60.00)	(23.33)		(16.66)	(100)
Total	32	17	2	9	60
	(53.33)	(28.33)	(3.33)	(15.00)	(100)

Note: Percentages are given in parenthesis.

Table shows that more than half of the respondents favoured their children to marry according to their own choices. Out of 28.33 per cent respondents who opposed this idea, majority were the males. Only two of the respondents favoured this for men but not for the women. Nine of them were of the view that they had no problem if the choice of the marriage partner would be according to their family and caste.

Coming to the question of give and take of dowry in marriages, Chanana (1996) did a very significant study. According to her 'despite generalized disapproval almost every one concurred that dowry should continue but only within limits. It should be given according to one's capacity without its exploitative dimensions. It helped in setting up the household of the daughter.' She further said that 'on the plane of sentiments, dowry was a compensation of the child's loss of membership of the family and the associated rights for it was just a chance that she was born a girl and not a boy' (Chanana, 1996).

The system of give and take of dowry was a common practice in Punjab, especially among the Jat Sikhs. The son inherited all the property, and the daughter normally was not given any share of the ancestral property. Dowry could be seen as being given in lieu of this inheritance to compensate for the passing of all landed property to the male heir.

Table 5.7

Ideas Regarding Dowry

Resp.	Should not be there	No demands/ Wishes of parents	Yes	No Idea	Total
Male	18	10	–	2	30
	(60.00)	(33.33)	–	(6.66)	(100)
Female	18	12	–	–	30
	(60.00)	(40.00)	–	–	(100)
Total	36	22	–	2	60
	(60.00)	(36.66)	–	(3.33)	(100)

Note: Percentages are given in parenthesis.

The table reveals that a majority of the respondents disapproved the idea of the system of give and take of dowry. It was of great importance to note that both the males and the females were in equal number who disapproved of this idea. While 36.66 per cent said that the parents should give whatever they wanted to give to their daughters, and it should not be demanded. Only two of the respondents did not respond to this as they had no idea about this.

In past, there used to be a tendency of marrying the girls at young age. Now changes can be seen in this aspect due to education of women; their emancipation and legislation have all contributed to an increase in the age at marriage of the girls.

Table 5.8

Appropriate Age for Girls to Marry

Resp.	18–21 Yrs	22–24 Yrs	25 and above	Total
Male	9	20	1	30
	(30.00)	(66.66)	(3.33)	(100)
Female	4	16	10	30
	(13.33)	(53.33)	(33.33)	(100)
Total	13	36	11	60
	(21.66)	(60.00)	(18.33)	(100)

Note: Percentages are given in parenthesis.

The data reveals that only 21.66 per cent of the respondents agreed that eighteen to twenty-one years of age was the right age for girls to be married, and most of them were the male respondents. A majority of the respondents agreed that twenty-two to twenty-four years of age was the right age. While eleven of the respondents preferred twenty-five years and above for the girls to be married and almost all of them were women.

This shows that women with education and urbanisation preferred to get married at an older age so that they could have an identity of their own.

With change in time and occupation, there has been a change in the age at which boys get married these days. Traditionally, when agriculture was the only occupation, boys started working at an early age but had lot of free time to spend. In order to keep them busy, their parents got them married as to keep them away from addiction and laziness. But due to migration to urban areas and education, a trend of late marriages is seen nowadays among the boys also.

Table 5.9

Appropriate Age for Boys to Marry

Resp.	21–25 Yrs	26–28 Yrs	28 and above	Total
Male	3	24	3	30
	(10.00)	(80.00)	(10.00)	(100)
Female	–	19	11	30
	–	(63.33)	(36.66)	(100)
Total	3	43	14	60
	(10.00)	(71.66)	(23.33)	(100)

Note: Percentages are given in parenthesis.

The data (Table 5.9) reveals that only three men were of the view that boys should get married between twenty-one and twenty-five years of age. A majority of the respondents agreed to the age group of twenty-five to twenty-eight years. However, most of the women agreed to the age group of twenty-eight years and above. It is to be taken into consideration that as the women preferred a late marriage for the girls, so they preferred a later age for the boys to be married.

Coming to their question of gender equality, it becomes important to know what the males and females of the same community thought about the gender equality. As per the nature of this study, this question was of great significance in order to know about the self-perceptions of the respondents and had there been any changes due to urbanism in the thinking of the respondents.

Table 5.10

Ideas about Gender Equality

Resp.	Equal	Unequal	Equal but Society does not approve	Any one should be stronger	Total
Male	15	14	–	1	30
	(50.00)	(46.66)		(3.33)	(100)
Female	17	9	4	–	30
	(56.66)	(30.00)	(13.33)		(100)
Total	32	23	4	1	60
	(53.33)	(38.33)	(6.66)	(1.66)	(100)

The data reveals that a majority of the respondents believed in the equality of both the genders. Another 38.33 per cent respondent believed in the inequality of both the genders (females 30 per cent and males 46.66 per cent). Only four of women argued that they believed in the equality of the genders, but the society did not agree to this.

One of the men was of the view that any one of the genders had to be stronger.

SELF-IDENTITY ON THE BASIS OF GENDER

After knowing about the effects of the process of urbanisation and changing lifestyles, it becomes important to know the patterns of changing notions of identities, the qualities preferred in the spouse, the way they negotiated with their caste, class, and religious identities, and how Jats Sikhs in the urban context identify themselves on the basis of gender. All these questions are very significant for the study.

The respondents were asked to identify and rank themselves on the basis of gender.

Table 5.11

Identity on the Basis of Gender

Identity	First	Second	Third	Fourth	Fifth
Smart/handsome Beautiful Good looks	M = 1 (3.33) F = 11 (36.66) T = 12 (20.00)	M = 11 (36.66) F = - T = 11 (18.66)	M = 10 (33.33) F = 8 (26.66) T = 18 (30)	M = 6 (10) F = 7 (23.33) T = 13 (21.66)	M = 2 (6.66) F = 4 (13.33) T = 6 (10)
Well Educated	M = 2 (6.66) F = 10 (33.33) T = 12 (20.00)	M = 4 (13.33) F = 12 (40) T = 16 (26.66)	M = 12 (40) F = - T = 12 (20)	M = 9 (30) F = 7 (23.33) T = 16 (26.66)	M = 3 (10) F = 1 (3.33) T = 4 (6.66)
Professional	M = 6 (20.00) F = 4 (13.33) T = 10 (16.66)	M = 5 (16.66) F = 7 (23.33) T = 12 (20)	M = 3 (10) F = 2 (6.66) T = 5 (8.33)	M = 3 (10) F = 5 (16.66) T = 8 (13.33)	M = 8 (26.66) F = 17 (56.66) T = 25 (41.66)
Ideal type of man/woman	M = 6 (20) F = 3 (10) T = 9 (15.00)	M = 2 (6.66) F = 4 (13.33) T = 6 (10)	M = 3 (10) F = 11 (36.66) T = 14 (23.33)	M = 7 (23.33) F = 8 (26.66) T = 15 (25)	M = 12 (40) F = 4 (6.66) T = 16 (26.66)
Flexible/change according to the fashion/style time	M = 10 (33.33) F = 7 (23.33) T = 17 (28.33)	M = 6 (20) F = 10 (33.33) T = 16 (26.66)	M = 2 (6.66) F = 9 (30) T = 11 (18.33)	M = 5 (16.66) F = 5 (16.66) T = 10 (16.66)	M = 3 (10) F = 3 (10) T = 6 (10)

Note: M = Male; F = Female; T = Total

The table shows that when the first three identities as preferred were clubbed together, a majority of the women respondents identified themselves as flexible as they could change according to the fashion, style, and time. Then followed, being a smart, handsome, beautiful, and good-looking person. Education was placed on the third position by most of the men. An ideal type of man or woman was placed fourth by most of the women. The last identity pointed out by the respondents for themselves was of being a professional.

QUALITIES PREFERRED IN THE SPOUSE

After identifying themselves on the basis of gender, the next important thing that followed was to know about the qualities the urban Jats looked in while selecting or choosing their life partners. Thus, the following table shows the qualities preferred in the spouse as mentioned by the respondents. Again for the sake of convenience, the first three preferences were put together to get the high, middle, and low-preferred qualities.

The following table reveals that in the category of highly preferred qualities in the spouse, education, rich, belonging to a good family background, and having good looks were the topmost priority of the respondents. Education was preferred by most of the women and good looks by most of the men respondents. Regarding rich and good family background, 31.66 per cent were men and 23.33 per cent were women.

Table 5.12

Qualities Preferred in the Spouse

Qualities	First	Second	Third	Fourth	Fifth
Good looks	M = 12 (40) F = 4 (13.33) T = 16 (26.66)	M = 10 (33.33) F = 1 (3.33) T = 11 (18.33)	M = 3 (10) F = 5 (16.66) T = 8 (13.33)	M = 4 (13.33) F = 9 (30) T = 13 (21.66)	M = 2 (6.66) F = 5 (16.66) T = 7 (11.66)
Rich/with good family background	M = 6 (20) F = 1 (3.33) T = 7 (11.66)	M = 7 (23.33) F = 1 (3.33) T = 8 (13.33)	M = 6 (20) F = 12 (40) T = 18 (30)	M = 4 (13.33) F = 7 (23.33) T = 11 (18.33)	M = 4 (13.33) F = 4 (13.33) T = 8 (13.33)
Well educated	M = 7 (23.33) F = 14 (46.66) T = 21 (35)	M = 5 (16.66) F = 16 (53.33) T = 21 (35)	M = 10 (33.33) F = 2 (6.66) T = 12 (20)	M = 5 (16.66) F = - T = 5 (8.33)	M = 1 (3.33) F = - T = 1 (1.66)
Nuclear family	M = - F = 1 (3.33) T = 1 (1.66)	M = - F = 1 (3.33) T = 1 (1.66)	M = 3 (10) F = 7 (23.33) T = 10 (16.66)	M = 9 (30) F = - T = 9 (15)	M = 9 (30) F = 9 (30) T = 18 (30)
Working/own business	M = 1 (3.33) F = 5 (16.66) T = 6 (10)	M = 2 (6.66) F = 10 (33.33) T = 12 (10)	M = 2 (6.66) F = 8 (26.66) T = 10 (16.66)	M = - F = 6 (20) T = 6 (10)	M = 4 (13.33) F = 2 (6.66) T = 6 (10)
Govt. employee	M = – F = - T = -	M = 1 (3.33) F = 2 (6.66) T = 3 (5.00)	M = 1 (3.33) F = 3 (10) T = 4 (6.66)	M = 1 (3.33) F = - T = 1 (1.66)	M = - F = 5 (16.66) T = 5 (8.33)
Staying at home	M = – F = - T = -	M = 2 (6.66) F = - T = 2 (3.33)	M = 1 (3.33) F = - T = 1 (1.66)	M = 10 (33.33) F = 4 (13.33) T = 14 (23.33)	M = 7 (23.33) F = - T = 7 (11.66)
Good-natured/ understanding/ caring	M = 7 (23.33) F = 5 (16.66) T = 12 (20.00)	M = 2 (6.66) F = 4 (13.66) T = 6 (10)	M = - F = 1 (3.33) T = 1 (1.66)	M = – F = - T = -	M = - F = - T = -

Note: M = Male; F = Female; T = Total

In the middle preference group, qualities like the spouse having one's own business or working, good-natured, caring, and understanding were included. A majority of the females preferred a spouse who was working or who had a business of his own. Where good-natured, caring, understanding, and with brains was concerned, 31.66 per cent of the respondents mentioned this. This was pointed out by the respondents themselves when they were asked to mention any other quality they preferred in their spouse.

In the low category, belonging to a nuclear family and government employee were included. Some of the women agreed for a nuclear family of a spouse. A government employee was only preferred by women respondents. Only one of the female respondents wanted to get married to a NRI and thus preferred so.

It was also necessary to know about the most preferred identity for the respondents when they were in the villages and in the city, respectively. Thus, it was significant to know about their notions of self-identity, and it would help us in understanding the changes brought about in the identity when one moves out from a rural to an urban area.

The following table reveals that the most preferred identity among the Jats in their villages was that of being a male or a female.

This was followed by the identity of being a ruralite. A majority, that is, 55 per cent of the respondents (28.33 per cent males and 26.66 per cent female) agreed to this.

Table 5.13

Identity Preference for Self in the Village

Identity	First	Second	Third	Fourth	Fifth
Ruralistic	M = 14 (46.66)	M = 2 (6.66)	M = 1 (3.33)	M = -	M = -
	F = 7 (23.33)	F = 8 (26.66)	F = 1 (3.33)	F = 2 (6.66)	F = 2 (6.66)
	T = 21 (35)	T = 10 (16.66)	T = 2 (3.33)	T = 2 (3.33)	T = 2 (3.33)
Urban	M = 1 (3.33)	M = 4 (13.33)	M = -	M = 1 (3.33)	M = 11 (36.66)
	F = 2 (6.66)	F = 2 (6.66)	F = 6 (20)	F = 3 (10)	F = 4 (13.33)
	T = 3 (5)	T = 6 (10)	T = 6 (10)	T = 4 (6.66)	T = 15 (20)
Religion	M = -	M = -	M = 1 (3.33)	M = 4 (13.33)	M = 7 (23.33)
	F = 1 (3.33)	F = 2 (6.66)	F = 3 (10)	F = 2 (6.66)	F = 1 (3.33)
	T = 1 (1.66)	T = 2 (3.33)	T = 4 (6.66)	T = 6 (10)	T = 8 (13.33)
Caste	M = 3 (10)	M = 8 (26.66)	M = 4 (13.33)	M = 7 (23.33)	M = 1 (3.33)
	F = 4 (13.33)	F = 1 (3.33)	F = 5 (16.66)	F = 7 (23.33)	F = 8 (26.66)
	T = 7 (11.66)	T = 9 (15)	T = 9 (15)	T = 14 (23.33)	T = 9 (15)
Profession/ Occupation	M = 2 (6.66)	M = 2 (6.66)	M = 3 (10)	M = 2 (6.66)	M = 5 (16.66)
	F = 2 (6.66)	F = 3 (10)	F = 2 (6.66)	F = 8 (26.66)	F = 3 (10)
	T = 4 (6.66)	T = 5 (8.33)	T = 5 (8.33)	T = 10 (18.33)	T = 8 (13.33)
Male/female	M = -	M = 2 (6.66)	M = 9 (30)	M = 5 (16.66)	M = 1 (3.33)
	F = 8 (26.66)	F = 14 (46.66)	F = 2 (6.66)	F = -	F = 3 (10)
	T = 8 (13.33)	T = 16 (26.66)	T = 11 (18.33)	T = 5 (8.33)	T = 4 (6.66)
No. of acres of land	M = 5 (16.66)	M = 6 (20)	M = 9 (30)	M = 4 (13.33)	M = 2 (6.66)
	F = 3 (10)	F = -	F = 8 (26.66)	F = 6 (20)	F = 2 (6.66)
	T = 8 (13.33)	T = 6 (10)	T = 17 (28.33)	T = 10 (18.33)	T = 4 (6.66)

Note: M = Male; F = Female; T = Total

In the middle group, the self-identity on the basis of landownership and caste were included. The low-preferred self-identities consisted of being an urban or city-based followed by professional identity and then the religious identity. Residing in an urban area was preferred by 25 per cent respondents. While 23.33 per cent of the respondents identified themselves on the basis of their profession or occupation (males and females equal in number). The lowest-preferred identity was the religious identity. The remaining 8.33 per cent males and 6.66 per cent females were the ones who had never stayed for long enough in a village to be able to identify themselves in the rural surrounding.

The next thing that followed was the self-identity preferred in the city. How someone does identify oneself in urban context? This again was one of the most important questions to be answered for the purpose of this study. After putting the first three preferred identities together, the following results were infer red.

Table 5.14

Identity Preference for Self in the City

Identity	First	Second	Third	Fourth	Fifth
Ruralistic	M = 4 (13.33) F = 6 (20) T = 10 (16.66)	M = 2 (6.66) F = 8 (26.66) T = 10 (16.66)	M = 3 (10) F = 2 (6.66) T = 5 (8.33)	M = - F = 1 (3.33) T = 1 (1.66)	M = 2 (6.66) F = 1 (3.33) T = 3 (5)
Urban	M = 3 (10) F = 3 (10) T = 6 (10)	M = 5 (16.66) F = 6 (20) T = 11 (18.33)	M = 8 (26.66) F = 2 (6.66) T = 10 (16.66)	M = 3 (10) F = 4 (13.33) T = 7 (11.66)	M = 7 (23.33) F = 5 (16.66) T = 12 (20)
Religion	M = 1 (3.33) F = 1 (3.33) T = 2 (3.33)	M = 2 (6.66) F = 4 (13.33) T = 6 (10)	M = 5 (16.66) F = 3 (10) T = 8 (13.33)	M = 8 (26.66) F = 8 (26.66) T = 16 (26.66)	M = 2 (6.66) F = 7 (23.33) T = 9 (15)
Caste	M = 4 (13.33) F = 4 (13.33) T = 8 (13.33)	M = 10 (16.66) F = 2 (6.66) T = 12 (20)	M = 4 (13.33) F = 12 (40) T = 16 (26.66)	M = 2 (6.66) F = 6 (20) T = 8 (13.33)	M = 8 (26.66) F = 4 (13.33) T = 12 (20)
Profession/ Occupation	M = 13 (43.33) F = 3 (10) T = 17 (26.66)	M = 5 (16.66) F = 3 (10) T = 8 (13.33)	M = 3 (10) F = 12 (40) T = 15 (20)	M = 2 (6.66) F = 13 (43.33) T = 15 (20)	M = 2 (6.66) F = 3 (10) T = 5 (8.33)
Male/female	M = 1 (3.33) F = 14 (46.66) T = 15 (25)	M = 2 (6.66) F = 3 (10) T = 5 (8.33)	M = 1 (3.33) F = 6 (20) T = 7 (11.66)	M = 12 (40) F = - T = 12 (20)	M = 7 (23.33) F = 4 (13.33) T = 11 (18.33)
No. of acres of land	M = 3 (10) F = 4 (13.33) T = 7 (11.66)	M = 3 (10) F = - T = 3 (5)	M = 2 (6.66) F = 1 (3.33) T = 3 (5)	M = 7 (23.33) F = 1 (3.33) T = 8 (13.33)	M = 4 (13.33) F = 3 (10) T = 7 (11.66)

Note: M = Male; F = Female; T = Total

The table clearly shows that among the highly preferred identities in city, professional or occupational identity got the topmost position as 65 per cent of the respondents agreed to this. Caste identity came next as 60 per cent of the respondents agreed to this. Following that was the rural identity or having rural base and most of the women respondents agreed to this.

In the middle identity preference group, gender; urban, and religious identities were there. While 28.33 per cent of the respondents identified themselves on the basis of gender, and most of them were females. Belonging to an urban area came next with 28.33 per cent of the respondents. While for 26.66 per cent of the respondents, religious identity followed next.

In the lowest preference identity, only one identity was there, that is, on the basis of agricultural land. The respondents further stated that nobody bothered about landownership in the city.

CASTE IDENTITY IN CITY

The respondents were asked to identify themselves on the basis of caste or how much significance does caste holds for them.

Table 5.15

Caste Identity in City

Resp.	Less Sig.	More Sig.	Does not change	Total
Male	6	14	10	30
	(20.00)	(46.66)	(33.33)	(100)
Female	4	13	13	30
	(13.33)	(43.33)	(43.33)	(100)
Total	10	27	23	60
	(16.66)	(45.00)	(38.33)	(100)

Note: Percentages are given in parenthesis.

Sig. = Significant; Resp. = Respondent

The table reveals that 16.66 per cent of the respondents, mostly men, felt caste to be less significant identity in a city. For a large number of the respondents (45 per cent), caste identity was more significant in a city. For the remaining respondents, caste identity did not matter, or it did not undergo any change with migration to the city.

RELIGIOUS IDENTITY TOO MATTERS IN THE CITY

Table 5.16

Religious Identity in City

Resp.	Less Sig.	More Sig.	Does not change	No Opinion	Total
Male	5	8	16	1	30
	(16.66)	(26.66)	(53.33)	(1.33)	(100)
Female	3	18	8	1	30
	(10.00)	(60.00)	(26.66)	(3.33)	(100)
Total	8	26	24	2	60
	(13.33)	(43.33)	(40.00)	(3.33)	(100)

Note: Percentages are given in parenthesis.

Sig. = Significant; Rest. = Respondent

The table reveals that only for a small number of the respondents, religious identity was less significant in the city. A large number of the respondents, that is, 43.33 per cent of them agreed that it was most significant identity for them in urban areas. Another 40 per cent said that religions identity did not change for them in the city, and it was the same as in rural areas. A majority of males agreed to this. Only two of the respondents did not have any opinion on this.

As per the class identity in the city, one can see that people are more class conscious in the urban areas as compared to caste. This is one of most important feature of urban life as reported by a majority of the respondents.

Table 5.17

Class Identity in City

Resp.	Less Sig.	More Sig.	Does not change	Total
Male	6	12	10	30
	(20.00)	(40)	(33.33)	(100)
Female	–	18	12	30
	–	(60.00)	(40.00)	(100)
Total	6	32	22	60
	(10.00)	(53.66 66)	(36.66)	(100)

Note: Percentages are given in parenthesis.

Sig. = Significant; Rest. = Respondent

The table reveals that for only 10 per cent of the respondents, class identity was of less significance, and all were males who reported that they had never given it a thought. A majority of respondents, that is, 53.66 .66 per cent of them found class identity to be the most important identity in a city. Class identity remained the same in the city as well as in the village for 36.66 per cent of the respondents.

Thus, one can see that due to urbanisation and urbanism, many changes have come about among the Jat Sikhs in Chandigarh. They have diverse views regarding their self-identities. Their occupational preferences had also changed.

CHAPTER 6
CONCLUSIONS AND INFERENCES

Many changes have come about in the Punjab countryside as a consequence of the success of green revolution. Punjab has emerged as a leading state of the country in terms of per capita income. The success of the green revolution in Punjab has also produced a class of people who have surplus income and an aspiration for upward mobility. After having exhausted the venues available in the village, they begin to look outside the village, that is, towards the city for further mobility in the urban and middle-class occupation. A large number of educated people from rural area have been coming forward to take up jobs in government and semi-government institutions and departments or have started business in the towns and cities of the regions.

The city of Chandigarh with its modern architecture, scientific town planning, aesthetic, landscaping with a backdrop of the noble Shivalik range makes it an obvious attraction. It has a planned urban infrastructure to provide its resident with an ideal urban environment.

This study has been designed specifically to focus on the most significant category of migrants viz. the Jats Sikhs of Punjab in Chandigarh. They possess all the attributes of dominance, viz. ownership and control of land, numerical preponderance, a relatively high status, presence in army, police, bureaucracy, etc. The majority of Jat Sikhs belong to the rural areas of Punjab, and most of them are agriculturist. But as mentioned earlier, they have also been moving towards the urban areas, reflecting their upward social mobility.

The rich farmers with surplus money at hand find Chandigarh as an attractive choice for investment. The capitalist farmers have been investing money in showrooms, plots, transport, petrol pumps, liquor vends, cold storage, cinema, etc. Chandigarh also offers job opportunities and a good place for living.

This process of migration and mobility also has implications for their self and group identities. Kaur (1986) has argued that 'at the village level, Jats have never felt a threat to their identity; beyond the village, especially at the regional and national level, their concerns become the same as those of urban Sikhs'. When the Jats Sikhs migrate to the urban areas, due to mobility and urbanisation, they obviously experience a change in their lifestyle and self-perceptions regarding their identity. How do their views regarding occupations, profession, education, gender equality, and their self-perceptions regarding identity change, as a result of social mobility?

Though limited in scope and exploratory in nature, this study was envisaged to find answers to some of these questions. The study was carried out in Chandigarh during the month of May 2000 to May 2001. A total of sixty purposive case studies of Jat migrants were carried out. Most of the respondents were selected from the relatively better off economic background.

The analysis of their socio-economic characteristics revealed that the majority of the respondents were twenty-six to thirty years in age. Agriculture with some other business was the main occupation of a large majority of the respondents. Half of them still owned a house in some other cities of Punjab as well. A majority of the respondents had their permanent residential places in Chandigarh, and they also had their families staying with them.

Almost all of the respondents owned the basic assets required in cities as most of them identified themselves as belonging to the upper-middle or rich landlord classes. Most of them had only one earning head in the family, and these families also had one or two school-going children.

The data on the pattern and process of migration revealed that the majority of the respondents were the first-generation migrants. Most of them were from Malwa region of Punjab, and they did not think of going back to the village. Regarding the motivating factors for their migration to Chandigarh, the most important pull factor was education, either for self or for the children, and then followed job opportunities, business avenues, and modern urban lifestyle. Most of the women respondents got married and settled down in this city.

Coming to the rural links maintained by these migrants, almost all of the respondents still had agricultural land in their native villages, and half of them also had a house there. A majority of the respondents reported that their farms were taken care of by their other family members. Some of them had also leased out their farms on annual cash contract.

The Jat Sikhs are known to hold land close to their hearts. Land is a source of pride and prestige to them. A majority of the respondents had not sold any agricultural land during the last ten years nor did they buy any. In case of only one respondent, a good amount of land was sold off when he had to marry his sisters. Even those who had sold land, the money received were often reinvested in the land. They invariably bought cheaper lands, which helped them increase the size of their holdings. A majority of them continued to depend on the income from agriculture.

The respondents visited their village whenever they had time, and almost all of them had maintained contact and ties with their village and so did their children. But a large number of them agreed that they could never go back to the village at any stage of their life. They wanted their children to keep the village connections alive and carry on agriculture, at least as a side business.

Regarding the notions of rurality, the respondents mentioned many positive qualities of rural life. Most of them found rural people friendly, innocent, honest, simple, and they had a feeling of belongingness as their roots were in the villages. Most of them preferred the good clean environment, and they felt that the presence of the other family members was good for the development of their children. However, many negative features were also pointed out regarding rural life. Narrow mindedness, interference of others, lack of the basic amenities of life, career problems, family feuds, factionalism, casteism, distance from the urban areas, low status of women, and lack of employment were identified as the negative qualities of rural life. Urbanisation was one of the major pull factors of migration from the rural areas. As a result of mobility, Jat Sikhs had experienced many transformations. Education was another important factor responsible for migration. Thus, most of the respondents were either graduates or postgraduates with a considerable number of them being professionals. Thus one can see the changed ideas about education among the Jat Sikhs of Punjab as compared to what they were traditionally. A majority of the respondents were staying in

Chandigarh from the last five to ten years, and a large number of them were the residents of this city from the last sixteen to twenty years.

The most significant inference drawn out of this analysis was that there had been a change in preference in occupation among the Jat Sikhs in Chandigarh. Pettigrew (1975) had mentioned that the Jats despised the townsman as lacking in physical bravery. They also had an image of them as grasping greed and lacking in dignity. Kaur (1986) too argued that the Jat might be employed as a school teacher or serve in the military, but he saw his primary role as that of an agriculturalist.

The above-mentioned formulations do not seem to be true anymore at least in case of migrant respondents in Chandigarh. It was found that Jat Sikhs in Chandigarh had rather different occupational preferences. Jat Sikh today did not prefer agriculture as their first occupation. Their primary role as an agriculturalist has changed. Rather, business in a city has taken the topmost priority among the urban Jat Sikhs and agriculture the second position. Jodhka (1999) has rightly stated that 'agriculture does not enjoy the same charm in Punjabi culture as earlier due to recent crisis and spurt of suicides and no one today celebrates agriculture'. The data analysed also showed the same response as stated by Jodhka (1999).

Armed forces which were seen as one of the esteemed occupations have gone drastically down in preference and so has the legal profession and politics. All these occupations as mentioned by traditional views enjoyed the topmost positions earlier, and the Jats preferred only these occupations after agriculture. But it was clearly evident that with the process of urbanisation, there was a change in the ideas of the Jat Sikhs, and they were no longer the traditional rural agriculturalists. They were well educated, and their preferences were for professional job.

Coming to the notions of urban lifestyle, a majority of the respondents stated that city life was marked by a good lifestyle as all the basic amenities of life were available there. People were generally broad-minded and less interfering. The respondents had a good social circle. Occupational choices were more, and one could easily rise higher in life in a city. Women enjoyed more freedom. They were educated and had nuclear families. All these above were mentioned by the respondents. In the negative qualities, the first thing the respondents mentioned was diplomacy, sycophancy, and show off. People in the urban areas were much more status conscious, busy in the rat race, self-centred, unfriendly, and money-minded. In fact, people were more materialistic and believed in individualism. Most of the respondents found Chandigarh an expensive city compared with other cities. Overpopulation, slums, pollution, housing problems, lack of morality due to more media exposure, lack of jobs, slow but hectic life full of tensions, and power game as the city was full of bureaucrats were some of the other negative qualities mentioned by the respondents.

There was more awareness and flexibility in the attitudes concerning age at marriage, children choosing their own life partners, and the give and take of dowry. It was clearly evident from the data analysed in the previous chapters that majority of the women respondents agreed for a late marriage for girls and boys. They were not averse to self-choice marriages and were against the dowry system. Most of the respondents felt that both the genders were equal. Women in particular emphasised this point. This clearly showed that with education and changed lifestyles, women had become more aware of their status and wanted to be treated at par with men. Interestingly, the younger men also reported that women were equal to them.

As mentioned earlier, due to shift from the rural to urban areas, it became important to study the pattern of the changing notions of self-identities, the qualities they preferred in their spouses, and how the Jats negotiated with their caste, class, and religious identities in the city.

A majority of the respondents identified themselves as to be flexible, adjusting, and changing according to the fashion, time, and style. At the second level, they chose to identify themselves as 'smart, handsome, beautiful and good-looking'. Their levels of education as a source of identify come at number three. There were more women who chose to identify themselves as flexible and adjusting while the men preferred to identify themselves as smart and handsome and well educated.

Regarding the qualities preferred in the spouse, education, good-looking, and rich with good family background were placed on the top. Interestingly, education was preferred by a majority of women and good looks in a spouse by a majority of men. Rich with good family background was again reported by a majority of men.

The most preferred identities in the village were on the basis of gender and belonging to the village or being a ruralite. Some of the respondents had never stayed in the village for long enough to be able to identify themselves in the rural context. Religious identity was the lowest preferred self-identity in the village.

When asked about the self-identifies, they preferred to be identified with, the men respondents ranked profession/occupation at the top. The Jat Sikhs women wanted to be known by the identity of their being from a rural background.

However, in their everyday life in the city, caste was the most important source of identification, particularly for the men. Women respondents reported that their religion and class were the most significant identities.

Thus, to conclude, we can say that with the changes in the lifestyles and changing attitudes towards self-perception regarding identity, Jat Sikhs in Chandigarh were more caste and class-conscious as compared to religion. They preferred to be identified on the basis of class and caste in the urban context. The respondents did not seem to be facing any identity crisis in Chandigarh. They moved in their own social circle, that is, among the people belonging to their own social status. Their friends came from diverse caste and religious backgrounds. Given their class status, a large majority of them has little or no anxieties about their identities. They seem to have taken to the urban life well, and the city too had accepted them without any resistance.

BIBLIOGRAPHY AND REFERENCES

Balgopal. *An ideology of the Provisional propertied class.* EPW, Sept. 1987. Editor Sachin Chowdhary, Bombay Hitkari House.

Barrier, N.G. and Dusenberg, V.A. (1989). *The Sikh Diaspora.* New Delhi, Chanakya Publications. (p. 35).

Bhat, Chandrashekhar. (1984). *Ethnicity and mobility.* New Delhi, Concept Publishing Company. (p. 21–23)

Gill, Rajesh. (1991). *Social Change in Urban Periphery.* New Delhi, Allied Publishers Ltd, (p. 18–19).

Gill, S.S. (1985). 'Genesis of Punjab Problems', in Abida Saminddin (ed.) *The Punjab crisis: Challenges and Response.* Delhi Mittal.

Glazer, N. and Moynihan, D.P. (1975). *Beyond the Melting Pot,* Massachusetts, MIT press.

Hall, S. (1990). 'Cultural identity and Diaspora' in J. Rutherford (ed.) *Identity: Community, Culture, Difference.* London, Lawrance and Wishart.

Haralambos, M. (1980). *Sociology: Themes anPerspectives.* New Delhi, Oxford University Press.

Harris, Henry. (1995). *Identity Essay, Based on Herber Spencer Lectures*. Oxford, Oxford University Press.

Jeffery, Roger, Basu and Alka. (1996). *Girls Schooling, Women and Autonomy and Fertility Changes in South Asia*. New Delhi, Sage Publications. (p. 129).

Jodhka, S.S. (1999). 'Retuen of the Middle Class', Seminar 476, April, 1999.

Joshi, S.C. (1994). *Migration to a Metro Polis*. Jaipur, RBSA Publishers. (p. 34, 105).

Kaur, Ravinder. (1986), Jat Sikhs: a question of identity. *Contributions to Indian Sociology*, (20).

Mach, B.W. and Wesolowski, W. (1986). *Social Mobility and Social Structure*. New York, Routledge & Kegan Paul Inc. Mayer, K.B. (1995). *Class Society*. New York, Random House.

Oberoi, A.S. and Singh Manmohan, H.K. (1983). *Causes and consequences of Internal Migraion*. New Delhi, oxford university press.

Pandey, R. (1998). Modernization and Social Changes', in S.L. Sharma (ed.) *Concepts of Modernization*. New Delhi, Criterion Publicatioin. (p. 22)

Peterson, W. (1970). 'A General Typology of Migration' in C.J. Jansen (ed.). *Readings in Sociology of Migration.* Toronto, Pergamon. (p. 49–68).

Pettigrew, J. (1975). 'The Jats of Punjab' in Dipankar Gupta, (1991).

(ed.) **Social Stratification.** New Delhi, Oxford University Press.

S.W., Sucha Singh (1994). *Economic Development and Social Change in Punjab – Some Policy Issues.* Ludhiana, Eqbal Singh Memorial Trust.

Sharma, K.L. (1986). **Social Stratification in India.** New Delhi, Manohar Publications. (p. 35–44)

Shina, Vandana (Cf. EPW may 3, 1998).

Rayaprol, Aparna. (1997). **Negotiating Identities: Women in the Indian** Diaspora. Oxford, Oxford University Press.

Webber, Max. (1966). 'Class, Status and Party' in R. Bendix and S.M. Lipset (eds). *Class Status and Power.* New York, The Free Press (p. 21–28).

INTERVIEW SCHEDULE

I. Socio-Economic Background

I.1 Name of Respondent :

I.2 Age :

I.3 Gender :

I.4 Education

I.5 Family Occupation :

I.6 Socio-economic class :

   (a) Lower middle   (b) Middle   (c) Upper middle
   (d) Upper,   (e) Landlords (f) Farmers

I.7 Do you own a house here or in any other town of Punjab ? No. 1, 2, 3. If yes, where :

I.8 Members of the family (currently residing at the present house)

Relation with the Respondent	Age	Education	Occupation	Rural / Urban
1.				
2.				
3.				
4.				
5.				
6.				

I.9 Assets owned by the family (put '/' or 'X')

Assets	In the village house	In the town	Desirable
1. Tractor			
2. Car			
3. Motor-bike			
4. Dish-anteena			

5. VCR			
6. T.V.			
7. Video –Camera			
8. A.C.			
9. Washing machine			
10. Micro-Wave oven			
11. Fridge			
12. Cooking-Gas			
13. C-D Player			

II. Migration Status :

    2.1 Family history: (Place of origin, why, where, who first came and settled).

III. Motivating Factors for Migrations:

    3.1 Reasons for migration to Chandigarh.
- a) Higher Education.
- b) Children's education
- c) Job opportunities.
- d) Business
- e) Modern easy life style.
- f) Terrorism.
- g) All of them
- h) Any other reason.

IV. Contact with the Village :

    4.1 Information regarding house and land in the village.

    4.2 How is the land cultivated

    4.3 Sale and purchase of agricultural land during last 10 years –

    4.4 Extent of dependence on the income from land

4.5 How often do you visit your village

4.6 Do you plan to go to the village and settle down at some stage in your life?

4.7 Do you think your children would like to keep the village connections alive?

4.8 Would you like your children to carry on agriculture?

V. Notions of Rurality:

5.1 Changing attitudes towards village life:

(a) Identify five (5) positive things about the village life:-

i)

ii)

iii)

iv)

v)

(b) Identify 5 negative things:

i)

ii)

iii)

iv)

v)

VI. Changing attitudes towards Urban life :

6.1 (a) Identify 5 positive things about the urban life:-

i)

ii)

iii)

iv)

v)

(b) Identify 5 negative things:
   i)
   ii)
   iii)
   iv)
   v)

6.2 Rank your preference for occupations (Ideally)
   I. Agriculture
   II. Business in city
   III. Profession (Dr. Engineer, Research & Tech).
   IV. Armed Forces
   V. Legal profession
   VI. Bureaucracy (IAS, PCS, etc.)
   VII. Computers / Management
   VIII. Staying at home/ house wives.

VII. Attitudes towards Mate Selections :

7.1 Do you approve of your sons/ daughters to marry according to their own choice?

7.2 Ideas about the give and take of dowry?

7.3 According to you which age is the appropriate for girls and boys to get marries :

7.4 Qualities preferred in spouse (Rank them)
   i) Good Looks
   j) Rich with good family background
   k) Well educated
   l) Nuclear family
   m) Working / own business
   n) Govt. employee
   o) Any other

VIII. What is most important identity for you (Rank accordingly)
    i) Village based
    ii) City based
    iii) Religion
    iv) Caste
    v) Profession / Occupation
    vi) Male / Female
    vii) No. of acres of land.

IX. What are your ideas about gender equality?
    a) Equal
    b) Unequal
    c) No opinion
    d) Any other

X. Identify yourself on the basis of gender (Rank)
    i) Smart / handsome/ beautiful / good looking
    ii) Well educated
    iii) Professional
    iv) Ideal Type man / woman
    v) Flexible/ Change accordingly to the fashion style and time.

XI. When in a city which identity is most significant?

	Less Big	More big	Does not change	No opinion
Caste				
Religion				
Class				

www.ingramcontent.com/pod-product-compliance
Lightning Source LLC
Chambersburg PA
CBHW030819180526
45163CB00003B/1348